IT'S BEEN EMOTIONAL

Also by Vinnie Jones

Vinnie: The Autobiography

IT'S BEEN EMOTIONAL

VINNIE JONES

**SIMON &
SCHUSTER**

London · New York · Sydney · Toronto · New Delhi

A CBS COMPANY

First published in Great Britain by Simon & Schuster UK Ltd, 2013
This paperback edition published by Simon & Schuster UK Ltd, 2014
A CBS COMPANY

1 3 5 7 9 10 8 6 4 2

Simon & Schuster UK Ltd
1st Floor
222 Gray's Inn Road
London WC1X 8HB

www.simonandschuster.co.uk

Simon & Schuster Australia, Sydney
Simon & Schuster India, New Delhi

A CIP catalogue record for this book
is available from the British Library

ISBN: 978-1-47112-759-5
ebook ISBN: 978-1-47112-760-1

The author and publishers have made all reasonable efforts to contact copyright-
holders for permission, and apologise for any omissions or errors in the form
of credits given. Corrections may be made to future printings.

Typeset in the UK by M Rules
Printed and bound by CPI Group (UK) Ltd, Croydon, CR0 4YY

I dedicate this book to my awesome, beautiful wife Tanya, for being my rock always.

My two great children, Aaron and Kaley, for always having the best smiles. And to my manager, Alex Cole, and Jeff Schwartz, thanks for your loyalty towards myself and my family in Los Angeles.

Contents

Prologue

There is a recurring theme in my life.

Things are good, everyone is happy – then I go and shoot myself in the foot.

I must be the only person who wasn't lifted by the Olympic spirit in 2012. I should have been – I love sport and consider myself a proud Brit flying the flag for Queen and country overseas.

But I associate the Olympics with one of the worst summers of my life: in 1972. I was grounded for the entire summer by my old man when the police turned up on my doorstep pointing a finger at me when I was only eleven years old. Two of my best pals and I had found a rifle in the woods near my house in Bushey. I had gone rummaging around in my dad's office, where I wasn't supposed to go, looking for ammunition. I found some cartridges, which almost fitted, and off we went to the end of the garden to try out our new weapon. We were firing these bullets at pigeons, taking it in turns to have pot shots, totally oblivious of the distance the bullets would go. A bloke down the road had been out in his garden while we were firing the gun and the bullets were smacking off his roof and raining down on him. He called the police, knowing fine well who was responsible, and, the next thing we knew, the long arm of the law was making its first inquiries with Vincent Peter Jones.

My dad asked if I was responsible, and I made my first really big mistake with him: I lied. Had I come clean, it might have been a different story, but I tried to wriggle out. He gave me a proper hiding – something you would never get away with in this day and age. He leathered me, and grounded me for the entire summer. I couldn't play football with the lads and I just stayed in and watched the Munich Olympics on TV. I sickened myself with it and it has only ever reminded me of bad times. London 2012 brought it all flooding back – even after all these years. I had a dream setup where we were living and I spoiled it for myself by being a little rascal.

In my teenage years I ended up dossing on sofas with all my possessions in a black bin liner, falling out with people and then moving on. I found it hard to settle, always upping sticks after some confrontation or other where everything would explode with fists flying and fingers being pointed in my direction.

Then there was the football career with the discipline issues, biting a journalist on the nose, air rage, trouble with my neighbours and giving Paul Gascoigne – Gazza – a friendly squeeze, among all sorts of other scrapes. Some serious, some silly.

Since I moved to Hollywood, the highs have been incredible but, as has always been the case, my own actions have led to some devastating lows.

Prologue

Guy Ritchie directed my first film, *Lock, Stock and Two Smoking Barrels*, and he once told me a great story when he got into the whole Kabbalah religion thing.

Don't get me wrong: I'm not signed up or a practising member or anything. But he explained a principle that has given a discipline to my life over the last year or so.

It was about dogs.

Guy said, 'Right, VJ, I ain't going to sit here and preach about Kabbalah – you're the last person on the planet I would do that to. But there's one thing I want you to think about.'

He explained that, according to Kabbalah teachings, we all have a dog corresponding to our personality.

It sounds a bit off the wall, but it makes perfect sense when you think about it. I've always said in life we've got devils and angels – the devil on one shoulder, always urging you to go and have one more drink ('Just one more. It won't hurt!'), and the angel on the other shoulder saying, 'Go home. Get your head down and behave, Vin.'

So Guy said to me we've all got this dog – but mine just happens to be a really big bastard. A big, angry bastard at that, one I should have spent more time understanding how to keep under control.

As you will read in this book, I seem to do so well, then suddenly I will destroy myself.

There have been too many moments in my life when the dog has been controlling me. There is no excuse for a grown man to wake up handcuffed to a hospital bed. It has taken me to this point in my life, at forty-eight years old, to realise that I need to control the dog that lands me in hot water.

I can't tolerate that shit any more, or ending up in the nick with my head in my hands over some drama that puts my family through the mill. There have been spells where I thought I have had the dog well and truly tamed, but then I'll get complacent and he'll come crashing out of the kennel, foaming at the mouth, biting anyone who gets in the way.

I was nearly blinded in a pub fight. That was horrendous for us all to go through. More recently, I was on the front page of the papers again for some business in Russia that rocked my marriage and my entire existence with my family.

So, as you read this, I have virtually given up drinking alcohol. I've had enough of getting into a pickle.

Since the incident in Russia, I have come back to my home in California and I see a psychologist called Professor Victor Morton. For the first time, I am tackling head on the problems I have had all through my life.

I've sat and talked my life through with this guy and much of what I told him is in this book. He's not a shrink as far as I'm concerned, a nutty geezer or an alcoholic's guy. He's the top professor at University of California, Los Angels (UCLA), a top psychologist – I wouldn't be surprised if the most important people in California go to him. I've been going to see him once a week for eight months at the time I'm writing this, and we've got the dog at the back of the kennel.

For an alcoholic to combat his or her problems, he or she has to admit to his or her problems first. With me, I'm acknowledging my demons.

I've been trying to work out how much the breakup in my family at a really young age affected me. All those nights I was up listening to all the arguments at our house, Woodlands, in Bedmond; you don't ever forget that. It was a messy, messy divorce. I have been trying to detach myself from it because it was my dad Peter and mum Glenda's relationship that went wrong. They loved my sister Ann and me very much, so why am I trying to be part of that anguish all these years later?

I've always thought the first line of defence was attack. When I was criticised as a footballer, I took it personally and went on the offensive, big time. If I was criticised for a part in a film, I'd get angry and attack. Now, I see a different, more measured defence.

So I'm in a really good place. I have had three careers, two of which have been a huge success. I put my shift in on building sites, carrying the hod, but, looking back as I write this, I realise that my acting and football achievements are something I am deeply proud of.

Getting into films, in particular, is something that I still have to pinch myself about. I honestly never thought this life I have had would be possible – especially in the depths of despair, when I found myself staring down the barrel of my own gun in the woods near my home.

Instead, I gritted my teeth, and as my dear friend John Fashanu says, 'The harder Vinnie works, the luckier he gets.'

The first movie I ever went to see was *Planet of the Apes*. My uncle took me to the Watford cinema – I think it was an Odeon – when I was about eight or nine. We were about a third of the way up the cinema, so still close to the screen, and exactly four seats in. At the time *Tomorrow's World* was a big TV programme and I remember being blown away by some of the talk about future technology. That programme, combined with apes talking on screen, really made a mark on me. I was convinced by the film that one day we would all be talking to apes! I think it's fair to say I was a bit of a dreamer at times.

The cinema made a huge impact, even though football was always my first love. When it came to films, I was into the big westerns – cowboys and Indians. I loved *Dracula*, too. I remember it vividly watching the 1930s version in black and white. Later, my wife Tanya – or Tans – and I would go to the Galleria cinema in Hatfield. We went to see some great films – and some howlers too. We saw a couple of *Carry On* films there – not exactly memorable ones, either.

I still can't believe that, after nearly fifteen years in the acting game, I have been up on that big screen in more than sixty films. It's the same feeling I used to get when I was on *Match of the Day* on a Saturday night. Nothing makes me smile more than giggling in the cinema with Tanya, giving her a gentle nudge in the ribs as I'm about to walk into a scene. It's magical – and I cherish every single second I have been able to do that. You see, you never got much of a reception walking onto a building site in the morning. And, later, it wasn't always the reception you would want, being hammered with coins, or blinded by lasers at some games, when you bowled onto the pitch as a professional footballer at a particularly intimidating away ground on a cold and horrible Saturday afternoon.

I've been making movies almost as long as I played professional football. Neither career has been short of drama – although you could argue I should have saved the drama for the second half of it.

Prologue

I spoke to Guy again recently and he reminded me that my dog is too big to tame completely. I get that, but, if I keep him sweet and read the warning signs, I've got a good chance of avoiding World War III.

As I'm sitting here now, I'm in full control. At the moment I just need a bit of help, and Victor is doing that. I come out from seeing him and it's like losing three stone. I step out of his office, get in the car, close the door and go, 'Phew!' I often feel like I could go straight to sleep because all that bad energy is out of me.

Bullet Tooth Tony from *Snatch* is one of the most famous characters I've played. There is a scene where Lennie James's and Robbie Gee's characters, holding replica guns, confront him. I give a big speech, as a cold-hearted killer sensing their weakness.

That situation with Tony is exactly how I face my dog. I have to be strong enough and, with Victor's help, I'm confident of chalking up another victory off the pitch.

One thing is for sure, and it's tattooed on my lower back as a reminder: it's been emotional.

1

Early Years

My life's been defined by coincidences, ironies, premonitions –
and that feeling I mentioned about a guardian angel sitting on
my shoulder.

Most childhood memories are black or white, good or bad,
happy or sad. And there doesn't seem to be much middle ground.

My mum Glenda was from Trowbridge in Wiltshire. In her
teenage years she moved to Watford, where she met my dad.

My dad Peter had started out in the heating-and-plumbing
trade, he was a workaholic, giving the pub a swerve to crack on with
building his own business. Going out on the town meant nothing
to him. It was all about shooting and fishing to him, something
he transferred to me – and I still love the great outdoors.

It began for me – Vincent Peter Jones – born on 5 January 1965
in Hospital in Watford. The ward where I took my first breath

overlooked Vicarage Road, the home of Watford Football Club and the team I supported as a boy. My granddad, Arthur, used to stand in the same place at Vicarage Road for every Watford home tie. He was there, twelve steps up and just a few rows down from the tea hut. We would go and get him a cuppa and take it back down to him. He absolutely loved his sport – he was always betting on the horses or talking football. I was only little but I found him fascinating. Ironically, years later, Watford were to knock me back from a professional contract because I wasn't 'big enough' to be a footballer.

The first few years it was all a bit cramped and full of house moves – some for the better, some not so good.

My folks shared a home on Queen's Road in Watford with another family – two rooms, a communal kitchen and shared bathroom. That's where the first big coincidence kicked in. When I played for Wimbledon I found out that the boss at the time, Joe Kinnear's mum had once lived there too.

The first place I really remember was Coldharbour Lane in Watford when I was about three years old. It was another shared house but we had a bit more room. We also had two Jack Russells – Titchy and Perky. I've been living with dogs around the house ever since.

I can picture my dad coming home and cleaning his gun, getting ready to go shooting in the countryside. Mum brought us up, as Dad was always working. When he wasn't, he was out shooting.

At one time dad had a pigeon hide in Chorleywood. The M25 now runs through where it used to be and it would turn my head every time I drove to training on the way from Hemel to

Wimbledon. I still get shivers when I think back to the first time I got to squeeze a trigger down there, on a 12-bore shotgun as I got to shoot my first pigeon – with my dad taking me through it every step of the way. We had a flask with us and a packed lunch. When I fired the shot, after my dad had positioned me carefully around the gun, teaching me how to hold it, I went flying – sending coffee everywhere. But I still hit the target. We were rolling around laughing afterwards. I wanted to keep that pigeon as a trophy – to stuff it and have it as a reminder of the first I ever shot, but I never did.

We moved to a house in Newhouse Crescent in Garston on the outskirts of Watford when Ann was born. Dad had two green vans for his work, all old-fashioned with big round headlights. The house had big bushes outside, with mauve flowers, and I spent hours catching butterflies. I had a fishing net and it took real skill to snare them on the move.

I'd started kicking a ball around when I was five. I was always competitive, even back then – whether it was about catching red admiral butterflies or scoring goals. Looking back on them now, I see they were really happy days.

I don't remember having a TV or any of our neighbours having one back then. It's mad – now I've got one in nearly every room, as well as smartphones, tablets, you name it. We all just used to play out. Or, if it was bucketing down, we'd go from house to house and make our own entertainment. I got a space hopper one Christmas and it was the toy nearly everyone wanted to have a shot on. Come to think of it, there were a few fights over it – the first of many for me.

Our next move was to 147 Lower Paddock Road in Bushey, Hertfordshire, perfect for me because it was across the street from the local recreation ground – the rec. Lights bordered the rec, so we could play even when it was dark, all thanks to the local council. My 'in time' was 8 p.m. My mum would come out the back door and shout, 'Vin-cent!'

Life was dominated by football and my dad brought back my first proper ball from holiday in Rimini, Italy. It was black and white and genuine leather. I loved that football. It was so precious we would rarely use it. My dad banned me from taking it to school, even though I was desperate to show it off, because he said the concrete would ruin it. Anyway, someone nicked it from the back garden and that was the end of that. Our garden had a big hedge, with a pub on the other side. Whoever nicked it must have jumped over, breaking my heart and all my mates' hearts at the same time. Whoever it was will never be forgotten. There is some bloke somewhere who nicked Vinnie Jones's first football and got away with it, but probably doesn't even know it to tell the tale.

My first game of proper football was at Oxhey Infants. I had to borrow a pair of boots from 'lost and found', which I remember were a pair of white Alan Balls, as advertised by our World Cup 1966 winner. They were a bit on the big side, but that was me officially in the football business! I did Bally proud with them too – I scored a hat-trick, we won and one of my three was slipped between the keeper's legs.

The old man was a builder by this point and spent a lot of time doing that house up. He'd even put a spiral staircase in, which not many kids could boast about having. It was ideal for me: my dad had converted the loft into a den and bedroom for me, wood-panelled and reached by its own ladder from the first floor. I was so proud of that room and that he'd taken all the trouble for me. I never wanted to let him down.

But one day I shattered my childhood peace of mind. A mistake I made at the age of seven taught me a painful life lesson – and earned me my first serious hiding from my dad.

He had an office in the house with a big wooden desk. We were supposed to be banned from in there, but would always nip in for a rummage around. I went in there one day, opened one of the drawers and it was stacked full of cash. Loads of wedge, dough like I'd never seen before.

It was the first time my dog had really emerged from the cage looking for some mischief.

I took a tenner right from the middle of one of the piles. Can you imagine what it felt like to a seven-year-old kid? It was like a lottery win. It felt like the easiest £100,000 scratch card. All I had to do was help myself. The mad thing was I wasn't nicking it for me. I used it to take all my mates to the sweetshop and treat them. I bought them everything, including penknives and toys, until the money ran out. I went back for more, but one of the teachers at Oxhey asked how little Jones could afford to be so generous and took me home to investigate. We arrived to a scene that would now look straight out of *The Bill*. My parents had discovered that some of the money had walked from Dad's desk and they'd called the police. The teacher told my mum, 'Vinnie's been coming to school with all this money in his pocket.' Later, the woman from the sweetshop rang to say I'd been buying up half the stock. The game was up.

Mum put me in my room to wait for Dad to come home and I sat there stewing. But never in a million years did I think he'd hit me. My stomach churned when I heard his voice downstairs. Dad was appalled by what I'd done and lost it. He gave me such a hiding – only with his hand, but a hiding all the same. I think the shock hurt me more than the pain. It certainly cured me of theft and I never did anything like that again. Well, the experience of that emotion has happened over and over again. I knew I shouldn't have done it and I didn't want to let the people I loved down – I just couldn't stop myself.

I know I hurt my parents deeply but, without intending to, they were to hurt me a few years later in the most difficult time of my life.

Some strange things happen in the mind of a child. When I was about seven I went through a spell of being terrified of dying. When I realised at some point everyone died I had a panic attack. I couldn't sleep and it genuinely upset me for a long time. Perhaps it was because everything was so perfect at the time and that was the one thing I feared. It's something I came to terms with later in life, but it was a phobia I carried around for a long time.

I also went through a terrible time when my dad bought a new house for us in Bedmond near Hemel Hempstead – Woodlands as it was called. It was a bungalow with about three-quarters of an acre of land – perfect for the family and our love of the outdoors, with forest on the one side and disused gravel pits on the other, where loads of local kids used to mess around.

The problem was, I couldn't come to terms with leaving Bushey and Lower Paddock Road. I was nine and had to leave my mates, my football and everything else I had made home on that patch. It was my empire and I went crackers at the idea of moving away. I thought at the time that, if I played up and caused trouble, the more likely my parents were to stay put – so I went berserk. I slashed the curtains and bedspreads in Mum and Dad's bedroom and my own. It made no difference. They were having none of it and really dug their heels in, but I really made it hard for them. Looking back, I realise it must have been awful for them to deal with. I think there is a part of me that has a tribal instinct and I didn't want to leave my sense of security. Even now I find myself inviting more and more people out for dinner when I am with Tanya. It drives her mad, but the hunter-gatherer thing is in my DNA.

I had this vivid dream around the time of the move. I was walking through a strange town and came across a football pitch. Bear in mind I knew nothing of the new place and its surroundings. I think I'd been there once when Mum and Dad were considering buying it, but I didn't want to know, and I can't remember giving that bungalow a second glance. But I dreamed of a place where I walked up a lane with no one around, crossed a big main road and walked round a council estate with little walls. Round the corner and down a narrow lane, and there it was on the left: a football pitch. A green chain-link fence all down one side, and the gap where you walked through had a single concrete bollard with a round top. I walked through the gap to the clubhouse and saw, across the pitch, a hedge and goalposts beyond. I saw all that, in the clearest detail, in the dream.

When we moved to Bedmond, the first day there my dad told

me to get out of the house and make friends. So off I went, up the lane with no one around, across the main Bedmond Road, past the little walls of the estate, round the corner and down Tom's Lane. By then I knew what I was going to find – the football pitch from the dream.

I still look back on that day and see it twice. The dream first, then how it was in reality. I have come to believe in fate. And, the way my life turned out, that house was somehow intended to happen. The whole area turned out to be football crazy.

There was a hedge around that pitch I found, and a couple of years later a professional footballer came to coach us. He had us all chipping the ball over that hedge and pointed in my direction. He said to John Cornell, our manager, 'That boy's head and shoulders above the rest. Let me know how he gets on.' That footballer was Dave 'Harry' Bassett, the man who signed me for Wimbledon and gave me the chance of a career in professional football. He's a lifelong friend and was a mentor during my career. He had a huge influence on me and shaped my professional life. See what I mean about premonitions and coincidences?

2

Kick-Off

Life in Woodlands soon felt like paradise. It was where my love of football and the outdoors really blossomed. But I was so unnerved by finding that the pitch from my dream existed in my neighbourhood that I avoided it at first.

Instead, I loitered around a green where a group of local kids would have kickabouts. One day on my way home I ended up joining in on the banter being thrown around. After about half an hour it kicked off properly and a fight broke out. There were three of us, throwing punches and kicks, but it wasn't that serious. I showed them the Jones boy wasn't to be messed around with. When it calmed down I came out with three new pals: Cal, Seamus and his brother Fran. Cal and Seamus became lifelong friends – I was best man at Cal's wedding and he has been there for some of the biggest nights of my life after football, too.

Despite the pals, school proved a problem. It was all a bit much for a little lad who hadn't wanted to move in the first place. I'd been at Bedmond Juniors less than a week when my parents were called in.

I'd been threatening to chuck bricks through the windows and told one teacher I wouldn't be there much longer because I was going to torch the place. Dad did his bit. He told the headmaster, Derek Heasman, about my trauma over the house move. And, when Dad told him I was mad on football, Heasman decided to use it to pacify me. It turned out he was the most fanatical Queens Park Rangers fan and the best PE master you could wish for.

Heasman and I used PE to take on the rest of the class – about fourteen or fifteen others. I don't recall our ever losing. We knew how to pass and move off the ball, then get it back – I learned from him how to make space for yourself on the pitch, one of the most important principles in the game. And I must have learned quickly, because I was the youngest to play for the Bedmond school team for years; I'm not sure if I still hold that honour. For years I was also the youngest to play for the Bedmond first team in the Herts County League.

But I was always in trouble, forever fighting and being sent to Heasman's office for his punishment – being whacked across the arse with a white plimsoll.

When my dad formed a Sunday-morning side with some other dads I turned out for the older side. It wasn't long before people from Watford and Hemel Hempstead had all heard of little Vince Jones.

Aged about nine, I was presented with a plastic man-of-the-match medal for playing against a team of boys from Garston, the village about five miles down the road. I lost the little base it stood on, but it had pride of place next to my FA Cup winner's medal for all the time I lived in England.

All the outsiders wanted me to play for them by then. But I've always been big on loyalty and stuck with the boys from my area, playing matches twice a day at weekends for the Bedmond Sports and Social Club teams.

It's the thing you hear about all the players who went on to make their mark on the game – you hear Wayne Rooney, for instance, finishing training with Everton, then playing for another few hours with his pals in the street. It was just like that for me.

The man who really got me going was John Cornell. He ended up as manager of Bedmond and became my biggest fan – and still is. When I was about eleven John gave me a hat-trick of hints about how to handle myself on the pitch. He said, 'Three tips for you, boy. When you knock an opponent over, act nice and pick him up – but pull under his armpits at the same time. When they squeal, just act innocent because they'll all be older than you. When a ball goes through to their keeper and he's holding it, just run up and knock it out of his hand. And third – if you're being marked too closely, reach back, grab him by the balls and twist. They won't mark you too close next time.' But John wasn't teaching me to cheat, just suggesting how a smaller lad could protect himself.

Eventually, I was chosen for Watford Boys. When I signed the blue schoolboy forms for Watford, aged twelve, Graham Taylor was manager, in the old Fourth Division. But the football was going well, I felt I was developing into a decent player, and there was the fishing and shooting as a hobby on the side. I say hobby, but it became an addiction in a way.

Work found its way onto my agenda when I was twelve or thirteen after I moved into secondary school at Langleybury. Dad was getting sick of my getting into scrapes so set me to work in the building game during the school holidays. It was his attempt to get me back on the straight and narrow. I wasn't into serious stuff – no joyriding or theft – just pranks and getting into fights. Pissing off folk in the neighbourhood, basically.

I hated the work, but did five days a week with my own timesheet and dad handing me money in cash. I felt special having fifteen quid while other kids got about two pounds in pocket money.

Then at thirteen my world caved in. For Vince Jones, that age was worse than unlucky: it was a disaster.

At that age the thought of your mum and dad divorcing was as horrifying as one of them dying. It soon became something I had to face because the arguments started – and went on for about a year. There was no escaping the sound of furious, raised voices, even in the sanctuary of my room.

The shit had hit the fan when a woman had appeared out of the blue and knocked on our door. She'd come out with the lot, telling Mum, 'I'm getting married but first I want to get this off my chest. I slept with Peter ten years ago, just the once. But I had to tell you.' You'd think she could have let sleeping dogs lie.

Dad had no idea what lay in store as he arrived home from

work that day, whistling – until he found Mum waiting at the door. She and Dad went at it hammer and tongs.

The hardest was when the rows raged on until four in the morning. I'd crouch at the top of the stairs, longing for it to stop and occasionally running into the room crying. Suddenly I felt I had to be the protective older brother to Ann. We'd fought like cats and dogs and never been close. But I would go into her room and cuddle her. Really I was crying out for her to cuddle me too. Our dreadful feeling of insecurity was made worse by the fact that Mum was sleeping upstairs and Dad downstairs. It turned my guts because it proved they were no longer really together.

Eventually, it was a good thing Mum left, except for the timing: she packed her stuff to leave the day before my fourteenth birthday. I begged her not to go, clinging onto her and shouting at the mates she had with her, 'Fuck off! Leave my mum alone.' It was no good. I finally released my grip. I had to let go.

The trouble at home had also been hurting my prospects with Watford Football Club. Things had been slipping because I was so tired staying up into the early hours listening to Mum and Dad's fierce arguments. But you're never prepared for bad news, even if you half expect it.

Bertie Mee, the former Arsenal manager whose team did the League and FA Cup double in 1971, was boss of the Watford youth setup. Clutching his folder, he told me, 'Vinnie, you treat life as a joke. Unfortunately, we think you're going to be too small. Nothing wrong with your football or your ability but your size is a problem.' I couldn't take that in. I thought that, if you could play, you should, but Watford seemed to have a thing about size mattering. Bertie tried to soften the blow by telling me I had the chance to go to Coventry, and that Tottenham had also shown interest. If Mum and Dad had been together, maybe I'd have pursued the 'other interest'.

Instead, the rest of my world collapsed. Dad had to move out of the Woodlands home he'd grafted like hell to get right so he could give Mum her share of the money. We moved into an old semi-detached labourer's house he bought from a farmer and my sister and I moved with him to the place, in Colney Heath, St Albans. Mum took a job in a nursing home, where she also lived.

My life had been building up nicely, brick by brick. Now my family, house and football dream had crumbled. It felt as if my paradise had been bulldozed.

The move to Colney Heath meant Ann and I had to go to a new school – Chancellor's in Brookmans Park. I started well, giving the school bully a beating and busting his nose when he decided to challenge the new boy. But I was good for nothing.

After just six weeks I couldn't be bothered. Not even football could get me back on track. I didn't tell anybody about my playing background or get stuck into games at break time.

When the time came to declare which exams I'd be taking I told teachers, 'None.' They knew it was pointless trying to change my mind, so released me from Chancellor's and I've never taken an exam in my life.

Dad had his own problems. He would come home at three or four in the morning and we communicated by leaving notes for each other. It was as if Ann and I were in the way. It wasn't that he'd stopped loving us. His new woman was pulling him away as far as she could. What shocked me the most was that he dumped his great passion – being captain of a pheasant shoot he organised. Just like my leaving football behind, I suppose.

Mum arrived once a week to take us out and I hated it. It was all so forced. Ann stayed close to Mum. But I didn't have a lot to do with her for a while, and, when she rang, I was always busy.

The divorce was horrific too. There was me, Dad, Nan and my auntie on one side of the room. Mum and a couple of her mates were on the other. Horrible. She wanted custody of my sister. When Dad eventually pointed out it was crucifying us, Mum dropped her custody claim.

I had to get out and do something different. So it was off to the building site. Up in the morning at the same time as my dad and away in the van. Humping bricks in a hod, digging, mixing cement – general builder's labourer, that was me at sixteen. And the fact that I could drive came in handy.

The old man needed time off when his hand went septic, so he handed me the keys to the van and there I was driving all round the Watford area without a licence. I had a laugh with the boys and worked a fiddle. We would stick ten bags of cement in the back of the van, then cover them with loads of other bits and bobs we were picking up. We would fill a form in with what we had taken, or claimed to have taken, without mentioning our 'bonus bags', which we would then go and sell. I wasn't worried about upsetting the old man with the blag – I think he was probably at it himself! Certainly, if he had been sound in the head at the time he would never have let me do it.

*

Time heals some wounds and Dad got better after he met Jenny Ambrose, his wife today. Mum got rid of all her friends and met Dave Hockney, now her husband. Dad spent the best part of a year building a large new house on some woods he'd bought and he was paying me £100 a week.

Peace didn't last long. I started mucking about at the building job so badly that Dad told me after he got himself together, 'Go and get a job, son.'

When the Youth Opportunities Scheme was introduced in the early 1980s Vinnie Jones was one of the first involved. Stacking supermarket shelves for £23.50 a week. Some opportunity!

I started to spend spare time at a cottage rented in the woods by a gamekeeper, Neil Robinson, and his wife Andrea. I met Neil when my old man advertised for a gamekeeper to help with the shoot. I remember the advert in the country-pursuits magazine: it insisted the applicant had to be married. Neil was twenty-eight and Andrea was only eighteen when they first showed up. It was only years later that we clocked that they weren't married at all at the time, but they had a pair of moody wedding rings to pull the wool over our eyes so they could get the job! They sneaked off to Reading and tied the knot one weekend years later, and tried to do it without our knowing.

I think my dad started to resent that maybe I looked at Neil as a father figure. The two of them had a furious row on our doorstep, with me yelling at my dad. He spun round and gave me a right-hander. It was the last time I went into that house. I gathered my stuff from my room – my clothes, football medals and stereo – and stuffed them into a couple of bin bags. I jumped into the Land Rover with Neil and went to his cottage – my life crammed into two black bin liners.

I told Neil I wanted a fresh start and his father got me into a boys' public school – Bradfield College near Reading. It was nothing to do with learning. It was to wash pots and pans.

I felt desolate and uneasy when I turned up at a strange school for my new job with all my worldly goods in one bin bag. The bursar explained what they expected and how they did things there, but the only words that stuck with me were, 'You'll be paid forty-two pounds for a six-day week, Sunday afternoons off.'

My room was on a long, creepy corridor, built on a corner and overlooking the sports field. It was bare when I went in – just a bed with covers. I tried to make it look like home, but didn't have enough with me to do the job. I carefully laid out everything from the bin bags. I lined up all my football medals on the win-dowsill and mantelpiece – medals from school days, Watford Boys, Man of the Match, Player of the Season, Top Goalscorer. I put out my stereo and a few records. That was the lot. That was all I had.

Washing pots wasn't too bad – it meant three cracking meals a day. After breakfast, lunch and dinner I could have any of the left-overs. In the evenings it was off to the Queen's Head. I was such a regular they put me in the pub darts team. They had a football team at the pub, too, but I didn't tell them I played.

If I wasn't in the Queen's Head, I'd be with Seamus and Cal, still my best mates. We started off as pals by having a scrap together, and things never really changed through the years. We had one massive punch-up when the M25 was being built. A lot of Northern lads came down to work on it, from Hull, Manchester and the like.

They would come into our pub, the Bell in Bedmond, and drink, which always ended in a scrap. There was one night we were in there having a beer and a skinhead bloke with boots and braces started a fight with us. Cal punched him and he never moved an inch. He was just rooted to the spot, ready to whack us all back. We did a runner, to Cal's brother's over the road. Big Joe was not a man to be messed with and he came out and backed us up in the alley between the houses. It really kicked off and punches were flying, but Big Joe dealt with the fella, and it was a reminder that there is always someone bigger and tougher than you out there.

I went to visit Cal recently, he's waiting for a heart transplant at the time of writing. He has been walking around with a battery pack, all wired up, to make sure his heart keeps ticking over. The drink has always been a problem for him, and that's something that we have tried to deal with over the years. During *X-Men: The Last Stand* – the third film in the series – he came to stay on set, and I helped get him sober.

I used a £500 summer-holiday pay advance to buy myself a 250 c.c. white Kawasaki motorbike and roared around without insurance – seems crazy, looking back. I'd also pierced my ear myself, with a needle I don't think I sterilised. I sat in my room slowly pushing it through the earlobe. The whole process took twenty minutes and I stuck a poxy fake stud in it that turned my ear grey and green.

Life seemed a breeze – I had my bike and my pub routine. It soon ended with a bang. I was hurtling along one of the country lanes on my bike, and round one of the bends there was a lorry headed for me. I swerved and ended up flying down a bank and through a barbed-wire fence.

My mum turned up when I was lying recovering from cuts and bruises and a wrecked wrist. I just said, 'I can't take all this any more.' She told me to get my gear together and put me in the car.

Mum was still living in the nursing home and I hadn't spoken to my dad in months. I ended up working with Neil and remember thinking that if a job came up gamekeeping, like him, I'd take it. If that had happened it's a good bet professional football, or Hollywood, would never have seen Vinnie Jones.

That dream ended when I got into drinking with my mate Cal. I left Neil's to live with him when our boozing and nightclubbing got out of hand. It constantly ended with us in bust-ups and sprinting away from police. By day we ran a roadside car-wash, and sitting outside in the sun wearing my shorts and Doc Marten boots was one of the best times of my life.

Once, we got back from work and found Cal's dad in shock. He told us, 'We're at war – this country's at war.' We thought it was World War III – nuclear weapons and all that. When the Falklands became a big talking point, one night Cal and I decided to join up to fight.

You do some stupid things at seventeen. We were serious about going to war just because we didn't fancy washing cars in winter. So we headed for the Army Recruitment Office in Watford.

We filled in all the necessary forms and the only thing that stopped us joining a battle somewhere in the South Atlantic was Cal's suspicious past. It was enough for the army to say no – and we'd made a pact we would only join together. So this escapade of ours ended quicker than we thought.

It's funny to think about how my son has gone on to serve Queen and country, considering my half-arsed effort at signing up back then. It's one of the reasons I'm so proud of Aaron, but that's for later.

Punch-ups stayed a regular occurrence when we hit the town. About thirty of us would meet at the Three Horseshoes in Garston, always by 7 p.m. and drinking bottles of Skol Special. We'd all pile off to another pub and then – wallop! Something would flare up and we'd end up in a scrap, at the New Penny in Watford or Bailey's nightclub. Occasionally we'd end up with stitches for our trouble. It went on like that for months. And I have to confess that I loved it at the time.

One night, after another fight, I got back to Cal's to find his dad outside brandishing a golf club. He yelled at me, 'There's your bag – now piss off.' He'd had enough.

Luckily for me, dad's sister Margaret lived nearby. I walked round with all my possessions – this time in a green football kitbag, and set up base on my latest 'home', her sofa. It couldn't go on like that, so Mum sorted me a room at one of her pals' places in Abbots Langley.

I hadn't spoken to my dad in nearly three years at that point. It was the Bedmond Under-18s manager, Johnny Moore, who had lost his father, who talked me into going to see him. It was difficult but in the end we just ended up talking about little things as if nothing had happened. I went back to work on the building sites with him but the arguments flared again. I wanted to show him I could stand on my own two feet, so went and worked for other firms, where I made another great pal, Mark Atwood.

Mark's dad, Peter, was head groundsman and gardener at the Masonic School in Bushey, which housed the United States International University (Europe), and he found me a job there.

Gardening was hellish in the wind and rain – but led to the greatest opportunity of my life.

I started playing football with the students, and the college formed a Sunday side, the IUE Flyers. It wasn't a bad little Sunday-morning outfit at all and we even made it into the Watford and District League. Football started dominating my thoughts again. I had a write-up in the local paper for two free kicks against Cockfosters – both screamers from outside the box, one in each half, whipping into the top corner.

I was mowing away, basking in my new-found glory, and suddenly I was saying a prayer. It was to my granddad, Arthur, Dad's father. He had died in October 1977 and I've never got over it. Our main contact had been watching football, and I just wish he could have seen me grow up to be a player. Cancer took thirteen months to kill him, after he'd been told it would take six. It ate away at his strong frame until he was a seven-stone skeleton. When he went, it was the first time I'd experienced the emptiness of a death; it had a profound effect on me as a child, and it was my first understanding of the word *grief*. He was special, granddad, so special that I believed for years that he was still in touch. I'm convinced he helped me out through my playing days. My prayers were always to him.

When I talked to him as I cut the grass at the Masonic School I was convinced he could hear every word above the mower. I prayed, 'I'd love to be a professional footballer, Granddad. Fourth Division, anything. One chance is all I need. If you can help.'

A week or two later Alan, the sports master, told me we'd have to get the football pitch shipshape because Wealdstone were coming to use it for preseason training.

Wealdstone! The top boys from the Gola League (now Conference), with their ex-pros from Fulham and Chelsea and all over. A big-time team, coming to me. And, when their manager Brian Hall later told me, 'You can join in if you like,' there was only one thing to say: 'Thank you, Granddad!'

I thought of something to impress when Brian gave me the nod to have a go with them – win the long cross-country training run. The one out in front would always be noticed, I thought. That's something I repeated at every opportunity throughout my playing career.

It must have worked. I started travelling with Wealdstone to other training venues, gagging to play. The patience paid off when I was given a few reserve games. I gave it all in those matches – until my most memorable day came at Wealdstone. Brian called and said, 'You've stuck at it and we want you to be part of the squad now.'

I'd got my shot. I was a semi-pro, on £28 a week – plus the odd £20 to cover expenses. I was being paid to play football, and I never looked back.

3

From Wealdstone to Wimbledon

Sticking on the Wealdstone gear was a big moment for me. My club blazer and tie became my pride and joy.

I'd stopped playing for Bedmond's first team but went back every Saturday night wearing club colours. I was a bit economical with the truth back then: I'd tell everyone I'd been a substitute, when I hadn't. It was a great feeling to hear everyone saying, 'Brilliant, keep it up.'

Life seemed back on track. Mum married Dave Hockney around this time, while Dad got married to Jenny. I was living with Johnny Moore, manager of Bedmond's Under-18s. He took me in when he saw I was living with a pal of my mum's after Cal's dad gave me the boot, waving the golf club as he sent me packing.

And I was back in the building game with my dad. He was

mainly doing house extensions with me doing the labouring. I was digging out, loading, hod-carrying and cement-mixing. There were times I bloody hated it. Most of the time, come to think of it.

At least Dad had caught the football bug again. He was happy to let me off work for training a couple of days a week and he and Jenny started coming to watch me in reserve team matches.

But it was an appalling tragedy that gave me another big break. A horrific thing happened to our first-team centre-half, Dennis Byatt who once played for Northampton. He lost his wife and baby during childbirth in hospital. During his time away from the club I was put in at centre-half. Dennis has become a lifelong friend. I'll never forget how those horrifying circumstances offered me the chance to take the first step in my career.

It was the season Wealdstone were going for both the Gola League and FA Trophy titles – aiming to be the first non-League side to do to the 'double'.

I ran into trouble way before they got anywhere near that goal, when I decided to fix myself a set of wheels. I'd passed my driving test aged nineteen, after years without a licence, by fluke. I took the test without insurance and tax and in a vehicle I'd never seen before. The examiner was a Mr Jones, another happy coincidence. I nearly failed when he asked me where I thought I should drive, and I replied, 'In the middle of the road.' I quickly corrected myself and told him I'd meant you should drive down the middle of your lane. He passed me even though there was a homemade disc under his nose insisting that the tax had been 'Applied for'. My mates had told me they'd show their arses in Harrods' window if I passed that day. I yelled at them after I got the nod from Mr Jones, 'Right, you tossers, up to Knightsbridge and let's see your backsides!'

Anyway, I bought myself a blue minivan from a friend for £110. Again, there was no tax, no insurance, nothing. I used it to take some mates to a nightclub and meet some birds. One of the lads threw a wobbly and I volunteered to take him home. My pal Dave Jefferson came with us and on the way back a police car drove past. I'd stuck to beers because I had training the next day. But I'd still had a load to drink and was worried about the lack of insurance and so on. I turned into a cul-de-sac to hide after spotting the cop car and sat with Dave for what seemed like ages, chatting and rolling fags. We could have left the motor and walked home in fifteen minutes – and should have. But we thought we were in the clear.

I reversed out of the drive but as we reached the end of the cul-de-sac two cop cars eased up – they were on me. It turned out an electrical shop had been turned over nearby – the window caved in and televisions nicked. When the police saw a gash on my foot I became prime suspect. I used to have this thing about socks. I only wear them if I have a suit on or I'm out shooting. I wasn't wearing any that night and a bit of aggro had kicked off at the nightclub. A glass had dropped on my foot and cut it. The cops didn't buy that and dragged us out of the car. Dave was slung in the back of one of their vehicles. I was handcuffed and chucked in another.

We were taken to Watford nick, where they kept us all night. The lads from CID kept coming into the cell and roughing us up a bit. They were convinced we'd done the electrical shop. I was done for drink-driving and they released me at ten o'clock in the morning. I had to be at Wealdstone for eleven o'clock for a match at Maidstone.

The coach was just about to pull out and I arrived looking like dog muck. My dad and Jenny were waiting there too. When they asked where I'd been it wasn't easy explaining how my preparation for the big game was a night without sleep, in the nick, and getting done for drink-driving.

The whole game was a disaster. My dad and Jenny had come to watch and I even managed to humiliate myself in the warm-up. I didn't have any kit with me, so I had to ask around the boys to see if I could borrow some boots in a size eight or eight and a half. The best I could get was a nine and a half, but I thought they would do. I went out and someone pinged a ball over to me, I brought it down and tried to smash it back. I struck the ball and the boot came flying straight off and went into the crowd. They were Lotto boots, a pair Lee Holmes had loaned to me – but they never saw the light of day again, lost in the crowd. I came on as a sub, and tried my best to look as if I wasn't hiding – but I was.

Three months later I represented myself in court. I was no Perry Mason. I was fined £180 and disqualified from driving for eighteen months.

Trouble followed me again: to Gateshead on a weekend, when we stayed over, playing two games within a few days. After the Saturday match the local boys didn't take kindly to the sight of me and the boys walking around a club with a couple of local girls. It kicked off outside among the locals, who were furious at being kept out by staff. Some of them were armed with bricks.

Our lads were in the hotel, but I went outside and battered two of the 'protesters'. The fight was kept quiet from the boss because the week before in Maidstone he'd told me I had to watch myself.

In the morning as we prepared to board the coach for training he noticed the blood on the forecourt. 'What the hell's gone off here?' he asked, probably knowing it involved me. The skipper, Paul Bowgett, took him to one side and said, 'There was some trouble last night, but it wasn't his fault. He didn't cause it, but he ended up giving a couple of lads a good hiding.'

The boss remembered that when he gave me a bollocking the day we played away against Kettering Town. I was due at the station at eight o'clock in the morning – but had no bloody alarm clock. A friend sped me to the station to find that the train and team had long gone. I was gripped by sheer panic and jumped on the wrong train. Fortunately, a bloke who noticed the blazer told me I was heading the wrong way. I jumped off at the next stop and, thanks to another couple of trains, I arrived before the team. Hally told me straight, 'You were finished if you hadn't showed up here. You'd better sort yourself out.' It gave me the kick up the backside I needed.

There was a specific moment in my Wealdstone career when I remember winning the rest of the squad over. We had got through to the third round proper of the FA Cup – at this point by far the biggest achievement of my career. We were playing Reading away and they had Kerry Dixon playing for them before his big move to Chelsea. They also had a big monster of a bloke who played centre-half for them – Hicks, I think he was called – and he was bossing the game at the back. I came on as a sub and absolutely buried this fella with a tackle. No mucking about –

bosh! I sorted him out. That was it from then on – they knew I wasn't to be messed with.

We were also the first non-League team to win the FA Trophy, and I played all the way through, including the semifinal against Enfield. I played at centre-half and right midfield in the match. It was a solid shift, nothing fancy or memorable, just professional – win your headers, win your tackles and try your best not to lose possession – but I never got picked for the final because Dennis Byatt had come back after his family tragedy.

The boys completed the Gola League–FA Trophy double – but I wasn't really part of the deal.

That night they held a party back at Wealdstone. They handed out team prizes to lads like me who'd been involved but not played in the games. There were three of us and we were each handed a handsome-looking carriage clock. I went straight into the toilets and smashed mine against the brick wall. I wasn't being a brat: I was just so gutted I wasn't involved. The clock meant nothing.

My driving ban was a pain with a new season coming up. I was determined to break into the side and needed to impress in training. But to do that I had to get there first. One of my mates had a brainwave: get a moped and a massive crash helmet to disguise myself from local coppers.

It's exactly what I did. My Honda 90 – deposit paid by mum and Dave – was a cross between a pedal cycle and motorbike. It had a maximum speed of 28–30 m.p.h., flat out, downhill, with wind behind. It took me the best part of an hour from Bedmond to Wealdstone and it was grim travelling in all weathers at no better than jogging pace, a parka jacket on my back and the biggest helmet you've ever seen.

It did the job, though. The local coppers didn't recognise me. Nobody did.

The Wealdstone boys naturally and regularly took the piss out of me on my moped.

There were other times when players would arrive in their fancy suits and I'd come in my building clobber – all mud stains and cement smears. But Brian Hall seemed impressed by my perseverance. I was completely taken aback when he told me there were League clubs taking an interest in me.

It was about that time I came of age – twenty-one, isn't it? Party time. And another scrap – the dog was well and truly in control of me at this point in my life. We had my birthday bash in St Albans, where Mum and Dave had set themselves up as landlords. The whole family were invited and everyone was aware it would be the first time Mum, Dad, Dave and Jenny would be together at the same time.

It was a bit tense to begin with but the party ended up being an icebreaker. Ice wasn't the only thing that got broken that night. A group of blokes gatecrashed my twenty-first. They barged in, I went over and that was it. We sorted them out. Me, Dad and Dave set about them. People started screaming, throwing punches, there were blokes tussling all over the shop and tables being flung about – a proper bar brawl. The police were called and order was restored, but the party was over.

I remember thinking there was one good thing to come out of that night: the sight of my dad and stepdad fighting on the same team!

My FA Cup debut was marked by something similar – though not as violent. I was sent on as a sub in an away tie with Reading.

My very first tackle triggered a fifteen-man set-to in the centre circle. I just went in on this fella and swear to this day it was a good tackle, but he got up and just went berserk at me. It all blew over, fortunately. We lost 1–0. But I wasn't sent off.

That happened for the first time in a match at Weymouth. They had a goalkeeper who was supposed to be a bit lairy. I went for a 50–50 ball as he tried to grab it. He took exception to the way I'd gone for the ball and I didn't like the way he'd reacted. Bang, bang. Other players dived in – and there were a few fists. The goalie and I were both sent off. Not that it ended there.

We had to walk through part of the crowd on our way off and I noticed my mate Steve Perkins – the nutcase of our team – sitting in the stand. As I made my way through some of the Weymouth supporters one of them spat in my face. Shades of Eric Cantona when he attacked a fan at Selhurst Park years ago! I was into the crowd after him and Steve – or Polly Perkins as we called him – was down from his seat and jumped in with me. I think we managed to whack the bloke a couple of times before we were pulled away and led down the tunnel.

Despite the distractions I held down a midfield place in the Wealdstone side during the 1985–6 season. I was happy enough with my progress until I heard some dressing-room chat about two players called Dibble and Nigel Johnson. It turned out that, during the summer months, they had been playing in Norway and Sweden. Hey, there could be a chance here, I thought. Sod the building game: this could be football full-time.

I'll mention another coincidence here. Guess who the go to bloke was who arranged it all. Dave 'Harry' Bassett, the one who had us chipping balls over the hedge at Bedmond, who at that point was the highly successful manager of Wimbledon.

I went to Hally and asked him if there was any chance I could be fixed up with a team abroad. I'd heard the banter: cash in hand, flat provided, free food and car, and I thought, This'll do me.

Bassett had heard of me. Derek French, Wimbledon's physio, had lived in our village years earlier. He'd told Bassett I was playing at Wealdstone. And Dave Kemp, Wimbledon's head scout, had seen me and told Bassett I had something. So when Brian Hall contacted Bassett about me he knew a little about who I was. I went to his house, where he was sitting with his wife Chris and the kids. Bassett said, 'I hear you'd like to go out to Sweden, and I can arrange it for you. Providing you can give me your word there'll be no fighting, no aggro, nothing.' I couldn't get the words out quickly enough: 'I won't mess it up. I swear Harry.'

A couple of weeks later, my first ever passport in hand, I was on the move again. I stuffed some jeans and boots in the bag, got down to London, and I was gone. Out from Heathrow and into Stockholm on 2 April 1986.

I must have been expecting something different from being abroad because I was a bit puzzled to find the weather just as cold as I'd left it in England – maybe even colder. I knew I was in a foreign country, though, when a geezer came up to me and said, 'Winee Djones? Winsent Peter Djones?' I must have looked a picture with my curly mop of hair, dodgy sheepskin jacket, work tracksuit and trainers. 'Winsent Peter Djones,' he said again. 'I am Burt Bustron, chairman of IFK Holmsund.' He must have been thinking, What's Swedish for 'What the bleedin' hell is this?'

We caught another plane to the north of Sweden. Once on board, Bustron assured me they were a 'very nice football club with big ambitions'. In fact, Holmsund were in the northern section of the Swedish Third Division. It turned out I was about to play for the equivalent of Bedmond first team. Maybe a bit higher than that, but nowhere near Wealdstone standards.

When the plane landed there was snow everywhere – four feet deep in most places. That was only part of the shock because after we'd marched across the tarmac I saw the welcome party – more than fifty reporters and interviewers with cameras and lights.

Bassett had told me to say I was on Wimbledon's books and I realised he'd done a right sales job. They were expecting a star. I told a string of porkies and felt guilty about it all. I said I was in the Wimbledon side and had come to Sweden to get experience and stay sharp. It was all over the papers the next morning – the long-awaited arrival of Vincent Peter Jones.

As I was driven to my apartment. The scenery was stunning, with rivers and lakes. I was in the back seat thinking, Bang on!

It got better. I was to live with Mark McNeil, a centre-forward once with Orient. And our apartment was beautiful – three bedrooms, massive lounge, kitchen, a nice little garden. And a brand-new Saab saloon for us to share. I thought I'd won the pools.

'We were told you like to go fishing,' the chairman announced. 'Well, we have a nice boat for you, with an engine.' The money didn't seem all that important by then. But it was good to hear I'd be paid £300 every fortnight, cash in hand.

Whatever sportswear I needed was to be chosen at a huge store and charged to the club's account. I knew then I had to make football my life. Having had a taste of this, I knew the prospect of returning to building sites was terrifying. So was the fear of not doing well and being sent home ahead of schedule.

We got down to business quickly. After being met at the airport, changing planes, doing a press conference, checking in at the apartment and kitting myself out at the sports shop, I made my debut.

They told me, 'We have our preseason game tonight, and we want you to play.' I could hardly refuse.

The venue was a grey, gravelly, all-weather pitch under floodlights. It was a freezing night, with eight-foot piles of snow bulldozed all around the place. The lads turned out to be a terrific bunch. But they looked a right picture to me first off – done up in tracksuit bottoms with long socks over the top, double shirts, gloves, and thick bobble hats. We won 6–0.

There were no players' bars or pubs like those I knew. The university disco once a week was about the only place to have a drink, so I gave up booze. I welcomed the new routine, though struggled with virtually twenty-four hours of daylight.

Mark and I turned into minor celebrities and I won the 'Player of the Week' award more times than anybody. Signing autographs at the supermarket was a new experience and I liked it. My dad liked seeing me do it too when I had him and Jenny out to Sweden.

We had a mighty cup game against Djurgården, one of the country's major clubs from its top division. This was like Manchester United playing Wealdstone away.

They should have beaten us 10–0 but they didn't reckon on the centre-half and the centre-forward from the same apartment.

Brian McDermott – the lad from Arsenal, now Leeds manager – was playing centre-forward for Djurgården and I marked him. My mate Mark McNeil went bang, bang, bang – wallop. He scored all our goals in a 4–2 win that seemed to confound the whole country. The national press said the next day we'd executed one of the biggest giant-slaying performances of all time in Swedish football.

Holmsund were knocked out in the semis but by then I had returned to England. They offered me £400 a week, tax paid, for the next season. I never signed that contract.

As soon as I stepped into that office they handed me a letter. It was from Harry Bassett, handwritten. It said, 'Jonah, heard you're doing brilliantly and that you're coming back next week. Link up with Frenchie on your return and come to Wimbledon for a trial.'

I had gone to Scandinavia pretending to play for Wimbledon, and come back to discover I actually was. It felt as if my life was about to change dramatically – which it did. But not even I could have imagined the course of footballing events that followed.

4

The Crazy Gang

Wimbledon had just been promoted to what was the First Division. It was an amazing leap from non-League to the very top level in a short space of time. And now I could be part of it.

I returned to England from Sweden with £1,200 – which I'd saved by sticking it in a drawer. One of the first things I did when I got back was buy my first 'posh' car – a £900 Ford Cortina.

I rang Harry Bassett to tell him how well things had gone and that I hadn't had a drink – a record I was to keep for almost a year after returning.

Bassett told me to get settled, give Derek French, the physio, a ring and come in on Monday. I never played for Wealdstone again.

My first match was at centre-half for the reserves at Orient and was nothing special. Then it was a night game at Feltham in a gale and driving rain – bloody horrible. An afternoon game during the third week of my trial changed things. It was against Brentford reserves at the training ground and Frenchie told them to stick me into midfield – which was my real position. I thought I was headed for the brush-off: 'Thanks, lad. We don't have an opening right now, but we'll keep you posted.' In other words, 'Don't call us, we'll call you.'

Then I scored two goals in that 3–1 win. I felt so comfortable in midfield, enjoying more freedom to run, winning all the headers. Something else happened in that match when Bassett and the others sat upstairs, watching through the office window. I took a throw-in. I picked up the ball and launched it almost forty yards. I heard the players gasp, 'Fucking hell!' They'd never seen a range like it and I didn't know I could do it, either. It was to become one of my trademarks.

The morning of my third week I was told Bassett wanted to see me. The cry went up from the other players: 'Go on, my son. Contract! Contract! Contract!' Bassett came straight out with it: 'Jonah, you're doing well, son. Gonna take a chance with you. I'm gonna sign you for one and a half years.'

It's hard to describe the feeling that came over me. I couldn't get any words out. I stood there stunned, gobsmacked, grateful and bewildered. I finally managed to gasp, 'Yeah, yeah, yeah,' nodding my head repeatedly.

I was given one and a half seasons to make a mark. Bassett warned, 'Make sure you work bloody hard.'

I was put on £150 a week plus £50 per goal and £50 per appearance in the first team.

I asked for a signing-on fee and Bassett snapped, 'No – I've given you your chance. You get in the first team and I'll look after you. Now fuck off.' End of negotiation.

Vinnie Jones was a full-time professional footballer with a club in the top division of the English game. Thanks again, Granddad.

I was picked to play against Nottingham Forest the following week. Bassett plucked out the team by telling the players he wanted to play to stick on blue bibs. The ones that didn't make it were in red. I was one of the lads in red until Bassett told Steve Galliers, a stocky little midfield player, to swap with me. I still look back and cringe at my first TV interview after it happened. London Weekend asked me how my debut came about. I suddenly developed a stutter and blabbed, 'Well, B-b-Bassett was g-giving out these blibs, blibs, b-blue bibs. And he g-g-gave m-me a b-blue one.'

Bassett lent me £150 to buy a suit – he insisted players wear them on match days and I didn't have one. I bought a dark-blue number and a nice white shirt to go with it. On the eve of my debut it was my pride and joy.

I was rooming with Wally Downes before the match. Wally, to this day, is one of my closest friends in the world. He has been there for me from day one in the game. It was my first glimpse at the law of the jungle that ruled Wimbledon, and the antics that earned us our Crazy Gang nickname.

Someone had his room turned over because he'd misplaced the room key. There were messages written in shaving foam on the mirror, bed linen ripped, towels dumped in a bath with the taps running. If you had your room targeted you were expected to sleep in it as it was. No calling the chambermaid. You had to get on with it. You were with Wimbledon now.

*

Tales of how I loved a punch-up at Wealdstone had delayed my initiation. Then the phone started ringing in the room I shared with Wally. He passed it to me and teammates were giving me encouragement like, 'First Division player, are we? Tosser. Shitting yourself yet?' Even Bassett and Frenchy were good enough to call. About 11 p.m. there were bangs at our door. I thought it was going to come off the hinges. Wally jumped up and in they piled, four players not involved in the match, and they had this old bird with them. I learned later she was a well-known, if not legendary, Nottingham Forest supporter nicknamed her Amazing Grace.

'Come on, Jonah,' they shouted at me. 'This is your initiation.'

'Piss off,' I told them. It was hilarious, looking back, but I became a scared young man. It was late and this was happening before the biggest day of my life. The boys sat 'Amazing' at the end of my bed and started removing her gear in front of the mirror. Off came her top, then her bra, and I shouted, 'No, no! Fuck off, the lot of you!' Wally was crying with laughter, tears streaming down his face. Amazing wanted a drink and they went and got a machine full of miniatures. She then rose to her feet and peeled off her remaining clobber, stood in front of the mirror and then looked at me. 'If you come anywhere near me . . .' I said. She didn't. She turned, sat on the end of the bed completely starkers, facing the mirror. And she started to sing, 'If you're happy and you know it clap your hands.' The lads were clapping and singing along. Then something snapped. There's a point where something 'goes' with me. The dog came out of the kennel. I grabbed her clothes and chucked them out of the door, and the lads could see I meant business, because they left too.

I still couldn't sleep, though. It was 1.30 in the morning and I was shaking. I'd imagined a nice early night in preparation for my big day. I'd ended up with a naked bird in my room and several choruses of 'If you're happy and you know it . . .'. Wally said to me afterwards that was Wimbledon. From that day, or night, I knew the score. It was the first time I ever thought of the saying, 'If you can't beat 'em, join 'em.' Wally was the first ever apprentice at Wimbledon and he knew the place inside out. Winning him over was the key to becoming a part of it, and we were as thick as thieves.

I got a few hours' sleep and breakfast. We got off the coach and were heading for the dressing rooms when we all stopped in our tracks. There, standing in the corridor, was the legend himself – Brian Clough. Nobody moved, and we filed sheepishly past him. If Cloughie could bring Wimbledon to a standstill without moving or saying a word, what damage would his team do to the First Division newcomers?

When we trotted out to warm up I was hit by a weird sensation. The further I went up the tunnel the more I seemed to be shrinking, physically and mentally. By the time I stepped onto the grass I felt about twelve inches tall. Then the shakes started. For some reason I started to run round the sides of the pitch. Like Forrest Gump. I was hoping to jog the fear out of my system.

The whole mood changed when I pulled on that first-team shirt – that No. 4. The only time that matched it was at Wembley in the FA Cup final the following season. I went from feeling four feet tall to twenty feet.

Our lads knew nothing about the Forest players. We were aware of Nigel Clough, their centre-forward, because of his old man. But as for Neil Webb and players tipped for England greatness, we hadn't a clue. And we didn't give a toss. They didn't know us, either – we were the surprise elements who had risen to the top, and that was our strength.

Intimidation was a big part of our ploy. Imagine Webb's feelings with me marking him and Wally shouting, 'You're going to get it today – right in the mouth.' When he held out his arms as if to say, 'What's all this? I'm just here to play football,' Wally kept on. 'First chance we get we'll do you,' he'd snarl. The keeper, Dave Beasant, would be saying the same to players in the goalmouth. The looks on their faces said it all: 'Who is this lot and what are they about?'

Not that it worked well that day. I was chasing Neil Webb everywhere and couldn't get near him. I kept thinking, I'm out of my depth here, I'm in the wrong place. Twenty-two minutes in, I punched the ball out of the way of Webb in desperation near the goalmouth to stop him scoring. Young Clough put away the penalty. I don't think I touched the ball that first forty-five minutes.

At half-time Sid Neal, who was sixty-five, told me to give him the shirt and that he could do a better job. That was that, I thought. The kit man was telling me I was in over my head. It would be back to Bedmond next week, done.

The second half wasn't much of an improvement, and I started my career in a 3–2 losing team.

I must have had to obtain thirty tickets for my second game, my home debut. I was part of a team about to play against the likes of Paul McGrath, Kevin Moran, Jesper Olsen, Remi Moses, Brian Robson and Frank Stapleton. It was Vinnie against Alex Ferguson's mighty Manchester United men from Old Trafford.

Unbelievable to most folk I knew – until they saw me coming out of the tunnel. Mum, Dad, the boys from Bedmond – everybody was there.

I was nervous, but keen to get started. There was no shrinking feeling this time. When the whistle went it was all about what I could do to make my team win. I wanted the ball.

About midway through the first half I went for a volley and caught it, sweet as a nut, only to see the ball come back off a post. I wanted some more of that!

Some books are boring, I know, when players drone on about countless goals in countless matches. But I make no apology about describing blow by blow the goal that sank Man United at Plough Lane – because it was mine.

We won a corner on the right. We knew Glyn Hodges would whip it in with his left foot, and we had players ready to attack at the near post, the far post and in the middle. I just stood there somewhere beyond the box when Brian Gayle said to me, 'You go first.' Me? This was only my second game for Wimbledon. And I was facing players I'd seen only in books or on the telly.

I started to take a run but realised I'd gone miles too soon and would probably be alongside Hodges by the time he struck the corner. I stopped, began to walk back and realised Kevin Moran had gone with me. I was actually being marked by Kevin Moran, Manchester United's Irish International. So I ran again, really ran, and the ball flew in from the right. I thought it was coming for my head – my head! I held Moran off with my left arm and threw my head at the ball. I didn't know where I was putting it, just thought, There's the goal, head towards the goal.' And *bosh*! Perfect contact. Remi Moses was guarding the post that I'd hit earlier with that volley. I remember he still had his hand on the post as the ball sped for the goal. He tried to head it and I thought he was going to knock it over the bar, but the power of my header knocked him back. The ball hit the roof of the net and poor old Remi landed on his backside. I had scored against Manchester United!

I didn't know what to do, how to react. I just ran and shook an arm in the air and looked for family and my mates in the crowd. I managed to see most of them before I disappeared under the heap of teammates who piled on me from all angles. It may seem strange, but at that moment I had another little prayer: 'Come on, Granddad, come on, please let it stay at one–nil.' And it did.

Afterwards there was bedlam in the dressing room. I had the peg next to John Fashanu and all the other players came over and took hold of me: 'You've done it, Jonah. We done Man United.' I could actually see the Wimbledon spirit everyone talked about.

The press asked for an interview and asked what I did before turning pro. 'I used to work with my dad on the buildings, digging out footings, hod-carrying, things like that,' I said.

The hod-carrier was the label that stuck from that day. It was something I had to live with for the rest of my career. The critics would seize on it when I messed up and cry, 'Get him back to hods where he belongs.'

I haven't liked it because it degrades many decent people – there's nothing wrong with carrying a hod.

I was having difficulty coming down to earth, though. It was as if the Man United match changed something. My family asked over drinks afterwards, 'Couldn't you hear us? We kept shouting at you, trying to attract your attention.' Suddenly I was made to feel different – not higher or better, but definitely different. After I played Manchester United it underlined that I had become a player.

And after that winner we played Chelsea away, winning 4–0, and I scored again. Sheffield Wednesday were seen off 3–0 at home, and I scored. I was on a roll.

Bassett had us shouting 'Power' during training so we appeared as invincible. He even had us practising surrounding and badgering the referee. That weird shrinking sensation never returned. I was feeling bigger and bigger but was also conscious of this Jekyll-and-Hyde thing inside me. I suppose that was when the dog started to enjoy making an appearance in public, too. If I put my hand on my heart, I have to admit I had no idea how to control myself back then.

The whole feeling at Wimbledon was frantic. We lived and played at 100 m.p.h. Hardly surprising, then, that trouble was just around the corner: Arsenal, at Plough Lane. Their player Graham Rix said something to the effect that we shouldn't even be sharing the same pitch and I whacked him. I was so caught up in everything. I could see Bassett going ballistic at the sideline. And the anger was not aimed at the referee.

My dog had raced out of the cage. I stayed in the dressing room asking why I'd done it but never came up with a satisfactory answer.

But Bassett was a vital part of the mischief-making that led to the players being known as the Crazy Gang, nationwide. Tony Stenson, sports reporter with the *Daily Mirror*, coined the name after a series of initiations and pranks, and it was used by all the media.

When we went to Portugal a few days before an FA Cup tie at Plough Lane, I was rooming with John Fashanu. Fash had become one of my best mates in the Crazy Gang – on and off the pitch. Off it, he always had some business on the go. He was one of the first lads I knew with a mobile phone when they were like massive bricks. He was on the bus one day and he tapped me on the shoulder and asked who were playing. I told him, 'Manchester City, Fash.' He would get on the phone and say, 'Hello, bubulah! My good friend Jonah has sorted you some tickets for the City game.' He was always at it. Years later he called me up asking about the movie business, and managed to talk himself into a film. He got the part of DJ Fash, playing records during a nightclub scene. He was a massive pest – demanded a huge fee, a trailer and everything else you could imagine. Needless to say, that was DJ Fash's last gig.

Dennis Wise was another really good mate in the Crazy Gang. We were driving down the M3, with me at the wheel, on the way back from a game, and we were all giving Wisey some stick at the time. He completely lost it and got a wire coat hanger around my neck when I was going down the fast lane, and started pulling on it! He was sitting right behind me and all the rest of the lads tried to help me, but he wouldn't let go. We ended up on the hard shoulder rolling around inside the car having a scrap between the four of us.

Big Sanch, Lawrie Sanchez, was on the receiving end of a lot of pranks by the lads in the early days at Wimbledon. We all used to charge our drinks to his room and he'd lose the plot when he came to pay the bill. There were a few occasions when it all got a bit heated: he and Dave Beasant shared a room and we would turn the place upside down. They never liked that.

Anyhow, back in the hotel in Portugal, Bassett turned his back for just long enough and his room key was away. We came up with a beauty this time: whatever wasn't screwed down in his room was removed. The bed, dressing table, television, chairs, lamps – the lot. All were lifted so they could be neatly assembled elsewhere. Everybody was there for the climax. When Bassett stepped out of the lift into the hotel lobby he found that his room had been reassembled there. Even his match notes were there, detailing players with specific tasks at set pieces. But the notes had slight adjustments – the kit man and Pat from the café were substituted for Bassett's original choices.

A few days later he really wound us up, telling us we were going to get beaten and constantly calling us 'poofs'. It sounds totally out of date and out of order now, but that was how it was back then. We ended up slaughtering Portsmouth so badly their manager Alan Ball said he was ashamed of his own team.

Bassett has been a mentor in my life. I couldn't be critical of him because he brought me into professional football and gave me the massive opportunity all kids beg for. Since I have lived in America, I haven't seen him so much, but he knows I am always on the end of the phone. During my football career, regardless of where I was playing, I knew I could call him up for advice and he'd give it to me – without pulling any punches.

Wimbledon had survived the First Division, a fantastic achievement for a little club. Bassett's priority was to make sure they stayed up at the top in that historic first season. I honestly believe that, if he had stayed, he could have changed Wimbledon's basic style of play to a more subtle passing game.

But it was not to be, not with Bassett, anyway. One morning during the summer break it was all over the back pages: 'Bassett goes to Watford.'

I thought it was the end of me and my world. Nobody but Bassett would put me in their team. I truly feared I would not be able to play for anyone else. He knew how I felt about his managerial style, he knew I was a Watford boy, but he hadn't asked me if I fancied going with him. And I was at a loss to explain why.

In fact, he invited me a couple of months later, asking me down to watch the game and have a chat. I gladly got down. I think they played Swindon that night and afterwards Bassett took me into the boardroom and said, 'I'd like you to meet Elton John.' If only the boys had seen me, shaking hands with Elton John, chairman of the club since 1976. It was my first real brush with celebrity. It's funny, looking back on it now, because I've crossed paths with Elt so many times over the years in all sorts of circumstances: at the Brit Awards or when he played for my neighbour Pete Sampras's wedding at his house in LA.

Anyway, this first meeting, he said, 'So you're a Watford boy?' We ended up talking for some time. I told him how my granddad had been a supporter at Vicarage Road and we chatted about Wimbledon's successful first season at top level, and of course about Harry Bassett. I was at ease with Elton because I could see he was so in love with Watford.

Harry said he'd have a word with Wimbledon's owner, Sam

Hammam, about buying me. As I was about to leave, Elton asked where I was going. I came out with the sort of thing you're not supposed to say to the club chairman: 'I'm away to the pub.'

He asked which pub. When I told him I drank at the Bell in Bedmond he asked, 'All right if I come with you?'

I thought it was one of Bassett's wind-ups – Elton John asking to drink with me at my local boozer. But he arranged for his driver to pick him up in the Roller and follow me up there. A few of the boys were in there but I didn't say anything the second I walked in because I wanted to wait until Elton had time to park up. As he walked into the bar I announced, 'Meet my new mate, lads!'

There were more open mouths than in a mass audition for *Oliver!*. Nobody said anything for a few minutes, but Elton broke the ice by beginning a football chat as if he had been a regular for years. He was just one of the lads – brilliant. Within ten minutes the pub was jam packed. He stayed for about an hour until the usual problem began: everyone and their aunt wanting autographs. He obliged umpteen times before coming across to me and saying, 'I think I'll shove off now.' It was only after he had gone that we discovered he'd left £50 behind the bar. Drinks for the boys. What a star!

It must give Elton a bit of a chuckle to see what became of that lad at Wimbledon. I find it funny to think about some of the kids who came through during my career and what happened to them. It's strange to think back to that time – it really felt as if something exciting was going to happen to me. Harry Bassett's departure wasn't a disaster at all: it was only the end of the beginning.

5

Gazza

It wasn't my football that really made me famous in the UK: it was *that picture* with Gazza.

The photo of me grabbing Paul Gascoigne by the bollocks was the moment I became a household name – but not really for the right reasons at the time. It was a bloke called Monte Fresco, a snapper for the *Mirror*, who took the offending shot. It's a shame, really, that he never really made any wedge out of it, because the newspaper owned the copyright. He did sort me out with a few of the original prints and they are all over the world now. Ridley Scott, Val Kilmer, Mickey Rourke, even the Brazilian footballer Ronaldo – they have all got one or come up and asked me about it.

It got me painted as one of the game's hard nuts at the time. Funny, because it wasn't done out of malice and I know that snap has always given me and Gazza a giggle when we look at it. We became good mates and my heart really goes out to him for what happened after his football career finished. But back then it really kicked off some massive headlines and all sorts of drama for both of us.

I tackled Gazza under the rule of new Wimbledon manager Bobby Gould. Just before I got to grips with Gascoigne's bollocks he'd made it his mission to clean up the club's Crazy Gang image.

I was still with the club because my proposed move to Watford with Bassett didn't meet with Wimbledon's agreement. It would probably have been the wrong time for me to go there, though. Bassett got released, Elton sold the club and I didn't see him again for years.

Bassett's departure from Wimbledon gave me a chance to jump in, anyway. It was the first time I really got to know the club's owner, Sam Hammam. I fancied my chances of a new contract, so I went straight to the top, to Sam's offices on Curzon Street in London. He upped my wages from £150 a week to £350. And this time there was a signing-on fee of £7,000.

I left Bedmond's Under-18s manager Johnny Moore's place and bought my first gaff. It was a three-bedroom semi in St Agnel's Lane, Hemel Hempstead – a joint venture with my mate Steve Robinson. He split the £48,000 asking price with me on a joint mortgage.

Bobby Gould arrived in 1987. He worked to change the club, to alter its controversial image and introduce an air of respectability (what a knob).

His efforts weren't helped when I bumped into Gazza. I'd heard there was a young lad up on Tyneside making a lot of headlines and getting the football community worked up.

At twenty, Paul Gascoigne was on the brink of the full England side – he was an outstanding midfield player but potentially one of the greatest footballers this country had ever produced. Gazza was really making his name. There have been big players who came through at a young age since – such as Ryan Giggs and Wayne Rooney – but neither of them had the same hype as Gazza as far as I am concerned.

Gouldy got one of the lads to play the role of Gazza in training, one of the lads who had a bit of skill. I think it was Andy Clement. He said, 'Right, Clemo. You're Gazza. Go where you want, get the ball, make runs forward and be creative.' Now, the last thing you wanted to do on a Monday or a Tuesday as a footballer was run around after some busy bastard from the reserves.

He was looking as good as Gazza and he was making a bit of a prat of me, so now the giggles start in training. The more Gouldy is screaming at me the more the lads are giggling. Clemo's trying to nutmeg me and all sorts, and I'm running round trying to lamp him, but he was a good lad and was really winding me up. After a week of the same drill in training every day, my fuse was about to blow. By Thursday Gouldy and I had a good old-fashioned square-up and I stormed off, screaming, 'Go and get some other fucker to run round after some fucking kid! I've come too far to be running round after some sixteen-year-old!' Me and Gouldy had a few rows along the way and he waited a long time to get his own back on me, but, when he did, he really put the knife in.

Our new coach, Don Howe, who was a fantastic football man with a great knowledge of the game, trained me how to mark Gazza out of the game by following him everywhere, playing him man to man. Don was the football man, and Gouldy was like the press officer.

Don calmed it all down and told me, 'This boy Gascoigne is something special. For this one game we want you to forget about your usual role in the team and mark this player man to man. It has to be done or we'll lose the game. He's that good.'

He pulled me over again and told me to prepare for the match by putting my feet up and thinking quietly about marking just one man – Gascoigne, No. 8.

I'm not sure I had ever thought about anything quietly before, but I did some thinking. When Saturday afternoon came I had put the Gouldy scrap behind me and had the job pretty much sorted in my head.

When I pulled up at the ground I saw a hell of a lot more cameras than usual outside. Gazza was coming! The photographers couldn't hold back. They were all over him.

All of a sudden something went *ping* in my head – I thought to myself, welcome to Plough Lane. As I warmed up I watched him constantly, flicking up the ball, catching it on his thigh. The photographers kept following him about and I thought, OK you prick, let's have it.

Hype like that hadn't been seen since George Best. David Beckham has had it since – girls running on the pitch with bunches of flowers for him, asking for autographs – and Gazza was loving it.

It was clear that this kid was special – double special. So I made up my mind that he was going nowhere. From the first whistle I was there. I eyeballed him. I was pumped up – teeth gritted, veins standing out on my neck. We hadn't been playing more than five minutes when he turned and asked, sheepishly, 'Are you all right, mate?'

'I'm all right, pal. But you'd better get used to this 'cos there's another eighty-five minutes of it coming your way.'

'Oh really,' Gazza grinned.

He asked me if I was his shadow and I was like, 'Too right, you fat bastard. I'm going to be here all day.'

Every time he got the ball I was on him. I was preventing him from doing his stuff. There were a few verbals, as there usually are in the course of the game. I told Gazza he was 'fat'.

The referee Mike Dimblebee had words with the pair of us occasionally. There was nothing vicious. The only time I was allowed to leave Gascoigne's side was to take my throw-in. But I had my doubts at the very first one. My instinct said, No, don't leave him.

So even when I was signalled to go and take the throw I shouted across to Gazza, 'wait there Fat boy! I'll be back in a minute.'

I was flying. I don't think Gascoigne could believe his eyes and ears. I noticed him glance across to the Newcastle bench with a bemused expression as if to ask, 'Where's this geezer come from? He's a fruit-and-nut, him.'

The more the game went on, the more deflated he became. Instead of trying to get away, he began marking me, standing close up. It was then that I remembered what John Cornell, my first ever manager at Bedmond, told me as a kid: '... if you're being marked too closely, reach back, grab him by the balls and twist. They won't mark you too close next time.'

Gazza was becoming frantic. At least that was how I saw it, because he was doing his best to get away from me, he started doing false runs, then he'd get tight as hell, trying to show I wasn't bothering him. I saw my chance had come with a free kick to us. I was facing the ball, he was right behind me, so close that he whispered, 'You're earning your £200 today, mate.'

'. . . reach back, grab him by the balls . . .'

I moved my left arm backwards and grabbed his knackers. As he tried to pull away, startled and shocked, I held on. Gazza screamed like a mother-fucker then.

He got on with the game after we 'parted' and at half time I heard Gazza had gone in to the dressing room in tears.

The game ended as a goalless draw and, even though there might have been a gesture or two out of place, I felt happy that I'd done my job.

I was still full of myself, still hyper, as I reached our dressing room. All the lads were high fiving me and shouting, 'Good job, Jonah!' A few minutes later I was heading for the bath when somebody shouted, 'Jonah, Jonah,' and Joe Dillon, our assistant kit man came through clutching a red rose.

He said, 'Mr Gascoigne would like you to accept this.' Brilliant! Where the hell he'd found the red rose I had no idea but it was a good gesture – worthy of a response.

I looked round for something to send in return and spotted the toilet brush on its stand. I grabbed it and said to Joe, 'Take that back for him, with my compliments.'

It was a funny end to a bloody good day. It had been a spur-of-the-moment thing, and I was proud of my performance.

What I didn't know was that the moment had been captured

on camera. I became very friendly with Monte Fresco in the years after. He told me the secret behind the snap. He'd heard me when I'd said to Gazza, 'Fat boy! Wait there. I'll be back in a minute.' Monte was just getting the camera ready and he said that was his tip-off. He risked his job that day because he took no pictures of the football. He gambled and followed me and Gazza everywhere we went.

So it was snapped – a couple of seconds of action to be frozen for a lifetime. And it was plastered all over the back pages. The reaction staggered me.

I'd just recently had bad press about giving an interview in which I'd admitted that, while up against Liverpool at Anfield, I told Kenny Dalglish, 'I'm going to rip off your head and shit in the hole'. That caused all sorts of aggro – serious problems for me on Merseyside, and the FA fined me two weeks wages.

I had already been developing a reputation as a tough guy. But it took the photograph of me grabbing Gazza for people to start to say, 'This bloke is a brick short of a barrowload.'

It wasn't so much that I was being portrayed as a hard man. But it got to me I was being painted as some kind of monster who was out of control, a law unto himself. Not really a footballer, they'd say. And, anyway, he came off a building site, so what do you expect? I hated that kind of thinking. What killed me about the Gazza incident was that I'd done such a good job in marking a skilful player out of the game for the benefit of my own team. I didn't regret doing it because I knew I had pleased Don Howe.

Bobby Gould tried to put it into perspective when he told the press after the game, 'I asked Vinnie to look after Gascoigne and he did. He did one hell of a job, so let's not be making him out to be a villain.' But he added, 'Perhaps Vinnie did some silly things at times, as well. We'll discuss those later.' But he rounded off with the words, 'He showed wonderful spirit out there.'

Looking back, I realise that I was probably more hyped up after that game than I was after winning the FA Cup. I came in and Don said, 'That's one of the best marking jobs I've seen in English football.' He was the head coach of the England squad at the time, so I was thinking, with all the press there for the frenzy of the Gazza show, that I would get an amazing write-up.

I used to love going to the pub with the boys on a Sunday lunchtime after a big game. I was firing up there and stopped off to get the papers at a newsagent to see if I got more than my usual four out of ten – a rating decided by a journalist who'd been at the game.

So I got the papers. I was totally shocked at the headlines: 'Psycho!'; 'Nasty!'; 'Crazy Vinnie!'; 'The ugly face of soccer'.

To this day, what was bloody heartbreaking for me was Don Howe's appraisal of my performance being wiped from history. He was somebody the football world would listen to and I know he told people high up in the game that my performance remained one of the best marking jobs he had ever seen.

In the game, everybody knew what I'd done that day, and I got a lot of respect for it. If the truth be told, in those days, by lunchtime all the journalists were fucking hammered.

Gazza came round to my house after he got transferred to Tottenham in 1988. He was living in a hotel at the time.

He came over to do a bit of clay-pigeon shooting. It was like something out of *Only Fools and Horses*. He had a shot at a clay, turned round to us and said, 'I'm doin' alreet, aren't I, lads?' and he turns round swinging a loaded double-barrelled shotgun in our direction. We've just hit the deck, and he's like, 'What's the matter, like?' I was screaming at him, 'Fucking point that gun away, you prat!' He pointed at the gun and said, 'What, this one? Let's see you grab me bollocks now!' I was on the ground with my old man and everybody else with our faces buried in the grass laughing.

He was mad on the outdoors, just like me, especially his fishing, and I got him out a bit.

We lost touch after he moved out of the hotel and bought his own place. Years later I saw him at the airport – I was going to LA for my first ever meeting with Jerry Bruckheimer. He looked like one of the airport staff. But Cheryl was there dolled up with about ten mates and family, all at his expense. It was ugly; he never looked as if he wanted to be there, and I felt sad for him.

I had my own troubles over the years, but he really got a rough ride – which you could argue was his own doing a lot of the time, but, I knew what he was going through. I see a lot of myself in him, and there have been a few times when I've phoned him to say, 'Keep your head up' or to say I was thinking about him when he was going through bad times.

Tans phoned me up once when I was away shooting a film. She told me to get on the Internet and look up a video of Gazza online. I logged on to the *Sun*'s website and watched the footage, which was really harrowing and devastating stuff. The worst thing about the video was hearing him struggle to tell that story about my grabbing his balls. We both must have told that story a million times each – but he couldn't get the words out and wasn't making any sense, just slurring his speech. I was gutted for him.

For a long time Gazza didn't play ball, with signing the pictures of that moment. If you've got one signed by both of us, it's probably worth a good few quid. It breaks my heart to say it, and I know guys like Ian Wright have said the same, but he has a long way to go to beat his demons. We both have. It's a scrap every day. A lot of people have a lot of love for him, but there will always be people around him who are a bad influence, and won't be happy until they've drained every penny out of him.

When he was in rehab in the US early in 2013, I tried to arrange to pay him a visit. It was a such a strict programme, though, and he wasn't allowed to see anyone.

A couple of years ago, I looked into making a documentary about battling his addictions. I was terrified anybody would find out at the time, because I didn't want anyone to think I was capitalising on his illness. I wanted to take him to Alaska, just the two of us, and live in the great outdoors with a couple of cameras. A really remote log cabin – no drink or drugs or anything he could get addicted to, just fresh air and me. We could do what we both love – fishing – for six weeks.

I still think it would have been a great show but it was on, then it was off – whoever was looking after him just couldn't see it. I had the idea with the best of intentions for Gazza. I thought it would be a way for him to earn a few quid and sort out some problems at the same time. As soon as one of his hangers-on mentioned that it sounded as if I was trying to cash in, that was it for me. No, thanks. I didn't ever want to be seen as a person cashing in on Gazza. It was never my motive. I just wanted to help. But, if that's how it was going to be seen, I decided I would take a back seat.

It's sad to say, but it does remind me a lot of the George Best situation. The Professional Footballers' Association and the players got involved and got him sorted out, but, ultimately, he wanted to carry on drinking. Just like Georgie, Gazza has got a massive disease and, unless he can sort a stable environment, he simply can't keep on the straight and narrow.

What were those people doing putting Gazza on the stage in the first place? That's the opposite of what he needs. I hear that just before this book was published in 2013 he was making progress, but the after-dinner-speaking circuit will always put temptation right in front of him, but that must be his main source of income, so it's a real catch-22 situation.

In my eyes it was disgusting seeing him carted on stage and being asked to tell a few stories. Those people have a lot to answer for.

I think the world of Gazza – I hope a signed picture of us at Plough Lane on that famous day doesn't have a sudden peak in value any time soon. There are not many weeks that go by when I don't think of him. Sometimes it's like having a twin, I can sense when he's having problems, then all of a sudden there it is in the papers or on the internet that he's relapsed. It always makes me sick to my stomach to think he's suffering.

6

FA Cup Victory

It wasn't all bad for me after the Gazza headlines. Something else had been ticking along for Wimbledon. A nice run of matches that were met with the familiar cry from John Fashanu: 'Put it in the mixer!'

The mixer – the phrase we coined for the long-ball game – started churning up a Cup run. Wimbledon, with their reputation for being scruffy, hard up, undertalented and overphysical, were on their way to Wembley.

The start of our 1988 FA Cup adventure was trouncing West Bromwich Albion 4–1. The victory gave us a fresh optimism. I started to wonder properly about the Cup after we went on and beat Mansfield 2–1. Something about that win set me thinking, Where next? Newcastle for a massive Cup tie exactly a fortnight later, that's where. Who could have written that script?

The game was billed as the big rematch between Vinnie and Gazza. Goudly tried to arrange a prematch photo with me and Gascoigne smiling, but Newcastle's manager Willie McFaul was having none of it.

Gazza was my responsibility again. He didn't get much of a kick, and I didn't need to grab him below or above his waistband to stop him. Final whistle, 3–1, and – bloody hell! – we're in the quarterfinals.

Watford next. The club that rejected me, but still my club at heart. Defender Eric Young equalised four minutes into the second half and Fash put us into the semifinals with a penalty. He placed the ball, took a couple of steps and dinked it – his normal routine, cool as you like.

There was nothing cool about our reaction. The semifinal was at White Hart Lane. Mick Harford scored first for Luton, then a Fash penalty was followed by my long throw to Dennis Wise, who bundled it in. We were screaming at each other, 'The FA Cup final! Come on!' I threw my shirt into the crowd and the rest is a blur of total happiness.

Back to reality, and we trained harder than we had all season the week before the final. We even trained twice on the Friday before the game, not finishing up until after six o'clock in the evening.

Then it was off to Cannizaro House, the plush hotel on Wimbledon Common. The laughs started when Gouldy announced he had a little present for all of us. His missus had knitted us each a doll of ourselves – in Wimbledon colours, blue and yellow, and wearing black boots. Mine was complete with a No. 4 on the back. We all collapsed when it came to the No. 9. She'd knitted Fash's doll in black. Brilliant.

It wasn't all laughs on the eve of the big day. A reporter came up to me and Fash in the hotel and told him he'd heard he was messing about with some woman. She'd done a story with the now defunct *News of the World* for the Sunday after the final. Fash told him he didn't know what he was on about. I warned him, 'You'd better get your arse out of here.'

When we went back to our room it was the first time I'd seen Fash lose his cool. He punched the door – proper solid oak – and he left a dent. The punch drove his knuckles into his hand. We called the physio Steve Allen. He was sure there was no break but the hand, which had ballooned, had to be bandaged.

Gouldy didn't want any distractions. He pulled a masterstroke of management and handed Fash a few quid and told him to get the boys together for a few jars. We went down the pub in Wimbledon. The lads soon started ribbing Fash, telling him the bird had better be a Page 3 type because his reputation would be in ruins if she was rough. It got things back on track. We were united again. As it turned out, there was a front-page story on the Sunday, some allegation of an affair, but it didn't cause Fash much hassle, he treated it as a setup and it soon blew over.

That night, I lay in bed, unable to drop off. I didn't want to let all those relatives and friends down who'd be turning up. Granddad. I needed a word with Granddad. I didn't ask him for a winner's medal. I just didn't want to cock up or be buried by Liverpool.

I was awake and out of bed by 6.30 a.m. Fash was still sound asleep and there was no waking him. I always say it was the butter-flies that woke me that morning – hundreds of them that had come in through the window and filled my body from head to toe. My palms started to sweat. I called Dennis Wise's room at 6.50 a.m., expecting a drowsy voice. He said he'd been up an hour. He was just as hyperactive as I was. We took a walk around the hotel grounds and I told him I wanted a haircut.

Gouldy must have sensed the nerves and took us on another walk in the grounds and told us to drop it down a gear or we'd be burned out before the match started.

I went for that haircut, though. On an impulse, I asked the barber to shave up both sides to meet the longer stuff – almost like a Mohican. My old man would never let me live it down. That haircut became quite famous at the time – David Beckham must have been paying attention – especially when I went to Leeds.

I was buzzing by the time we got on the coach.

We saw the Liverpool team leaving their hotel on the onboard TV. Liverpool, of course, at the time were a huge domestic and European powerhouse in football. You look at the way Manchester United dominated the domestic top flight for the last couple of decades under Sir Alex Ferguson (who retired in May 2013 and handed the reins to fellow Scot David Moyes). Well, Liverpool did it first and with serious swagger and self-belief. They had a presence. But on the TV on that bus they looked as if they were on their way to a funeral. There had been talk that they were bored, having been there and done it. We started to shout, 'They don't fancy it!'

We all looked dapper in our suits, some of us wearing the sprays of yellow and blue flowers I'd bought. The only colour we could see when we pulled up at Wembley was red. Liverpool supporters everywhere. 'Good old Wimbledon,' they were saying. They thought we were their whipping boys.

As we headed onto the pitch for a walkabout in our suits the feeling was good – the sweaty palms my only sense of pressure.

But the butterflies returned back in the dressing room when I hung up my suit and thought, The next time I put this on I'll have played in the 1988 FA Cup final.

We went into a huddle – 'Come on, let's do it' – as Don gave us instruction: 'Close them down, send them back at half-time needing to reshuffle.'

By the time I stepped out into that tunnel I felt twice my normal size. The Liverpool boys had come into the tunnel quietly. We came out roaring. 'This is ours today,' one of us shouted. 'Big-time Charlies,' I yelled at their lot. 'You're gonna get it out there.' Kenny Dalglish told them not to listen. The more it went on the bigger I felt as we marched towards the mouth of the tunnel.

There's nothing to match the sensation that hits you when you walk from the mouth of the tunnel. You see a huge horseshoe shape filled with tens of thousands of fans' faces and dazzling colour. It all seemed to be red and white.

We lined up and Princess Di filed along. I was hoping she'd stop and talk to me but she just said, 'Hello,' shook hands and that was it.

As the anthem blared out we stared down the Liverpool squad until they looked away uncomfortably.

I won't bore you with the tactical details but the key to beating Liverpool was preventing John Barnes and Steve McMahon winning the encounter in midfield.

I can't even tell you who kicked off. The first thing that springs to mind is Andy Thorn getting tied up with Peter Beardsley. John Barnes had a scoring chance and I went in shoulder to shoulder to sweep away the ball. He looked at me as if to say, 'You want it that much, do you?'

For twenty minutes we worked our socks off, we didn't let up the midfield, we shut them down.

Then McMahon had the ball. I started running at him and met him – wallop! Lovely. His legs went up in the air. I was on the ground looking up at him as he came down when he showed what a pro he was. Maybe it was just luck but as he landed he caught me with his elbow under my left eye. It split and bled and it still shows the mark sometimes. My lifelong reminder of a clash on the sacred turf! From then on, the Liverpool players had one eye on the ball and the other on our players every time they went in for a tackle. They didn't rise to the physical challenge.

Suddenly there was bedlam. A free kick to us from wide of the box. Alan Cork made his run, Lawrie Sanchez stood his ground and got in a header. I saw their goalie Bruce Grobbelaar transfixed. It was as if he had been set in stone. There was nothing he could do but look him up and down. The roar battered the eardrums. A goal, a bloody goal! We had scored! Wimbledon had scored at Wembley!

Half-time brought panic stations, because we were sure the only thing that would beat us was running out of steam. Don told us to wrap in cold towels to cool the blood.

Nothing could have cooled us off. Especially when referee Brian Hill gave Liverpool a penalty in the second half. We knew our goalie Dave Beasant had done his homework on John Aldridge's penalty kicks. He made history with the dive that brought the first ever penalty save in an FA Cup final. I was first over to grab him.

Everything became frantic. There were substitutions, and John Scales was off the bench. I shouted at him, 'Scalesy, where are you playing?' when he stood in front of me. He frowned and said, 'Don't know, Goudly said just roar about upfront.' Time was running out, and we held our 1–0 lead.

The final whistle in a Cup final you have won is the most beautiful sound imaginable. Fash and I were ecstatic. We all were. Andy Thorn jumped on Beasant's back. Gouldy came running on and jumped into my arms. The injured lads and those who hadn't played all joined us.

We clapped the Liverpool team as they went up for their losers' medals. Gouldy warned us, 'Be gentlemen and do the right thing.'

You grab a hat, a scarf, and shake as many hands as possible up those steps. A medal from Princess Di and a kiss from Sam Hammam. With no disrespect to either, you wished it had been the other way round.

The Liverpool players were shaking our hands but, when I made my way towards McMahon, he turned to walk off. Dalglish grabbed him by the arm and told him, 'Oi, shake his hand.' He shook it, but didn't look at me.

Then there were the photographs, the lap of honour, the elation. On the way round the lap of honour, as we all danced and sang and yelled, a steward stepped in and reminded us we couldn't go on the dog track. But when I saw my mates from Bedmond and Watford I used to play with I shoved the steward out of the way and roared over to the fence. They were all reaching through the fence, trying to touch my medal. And I thought, Shit, if I drop it . . . and stood back a bit. One of them told me Harry Bassett was in the gantry. He was doing some TV work and I grabbed the Cup and held it up. As Harry looked down I became all emotional. I welled up but screamed up at him, 'This is for you Harry. This should be yours.' And I pretended to throw it up to him. To the bloke who had given me the chance I had prayed for.

The atmosphere in the dressing room afterwards had to be experienced to be believed. Liverpool's was deathly quiet but ours was full blast. Photographs being taken everywhere, BBC commentator John Motson joining in and having a great time. The ghetto blaster at full volume.

All the other players were dressed and on the coach by the time Lawrie Sanchez and I came out of the bath. I left the dressing room stripped to the waist with just my trousers, shoes and socks on. I finished dressing on the coach with another blast of champagne.

Back at Plough Lane, the place was heaving. I was hit by what amounted to a rugby tackle from my old man. He spun me around and they were all there: my nan, my mum, my sister and loads more friends and family. We seemed to be swept along by a tide into a huge marquee for our party.

Dad had to leave the Plough Lane bash because he had invited everyone in Watford to a party in the barn at home. There were parties here, parties there, including one at the Venture pub in Hemel.

I eventually got to ours at about 1 a.m. Sam Hammam had invited his ballet friends along to the party. The place exploded when I arrived home, and I'd never seen so many tears in one place. Then I just sagged.

But the crowning glory, which all Wembley winners enjoy, was the bus tour on the Sunday. The mayor, the town-hall balcony, the thousands of people lining the route – fabulous memories that could never be repeated. Certainly for a lad who once paused while mowing grass and prayed for just one chance to be a professional footballer. Before getting on the bus I realised I'd somehow left my medal in the Venture. I phoned Eddie the landlord and said, 'Eddie, please tell me you've got my Cup final medal there.' He said, 'Oh, yeah, the boys have hung it up in the dartboard trophy cabinet.' I went in there that night and there it was, pinned up in the cabinet. It was a great moment, seeing my medal hanging up for all to see – it made me feel so proud. That medal had an unusual journey, it's fair to say, but more of that later.

There was only one way to end the perfect week: down at the Bell with all the Bedmond boys on the Sunday night. It was the start of more celebrations. They lasted another week.

I never thought it would be done again – the scale of that giant Cup final at Wembley. Wigan managed to do it, twenty-five years after us, by beating Manchester City and their multimillionaire squad, which was great to see, but the game has changed so much in that time. That game in 1988 was the springboard for it all, for me, and the tattoo I had done on my right leg is a reminder of a very special occasion only a lucky few British footballers can say they've enjoyed.

7

Transfers and Tantrums

The FA Cup comedown was brutal. We couldn't have had a worse start to Wimbledon's 1988–9 season as Cup holders. It started preseason. I don't know whether it was a favour to one of Gouldy's mates but we found ourselves playing a village team in Shanklin on the Isle of Wight at what seemed to be an annual fête in some park.

We trained hard as always but went out the night before and had a bit of banter with the local players. There were some bitter remarks aimed in my direction, along the theme of 'If *you've* made it as a footballer, *I* should be a footballer.' The difference was, they never had the heart, passion and determination – the attributes that carried me through.

You don't expect to land in it at a friendly on the Isle of Wight, but it happened. I went in after some geezer gave Dennis Wise a smack and there was a right bundle.

These things kept happening – I got tangled up, then ended up hating myself afterwards. The dog slipping off the lead yet again and giving out a bite.

I jumped up and was expecting the ref to wade in but instead he ran up and stuck a red card in my face – just me! And it was off for me.

They had put on tea and cakes after the game to thank Wimbledon for coming down. I was sitting chatting when Gouldy strode over and ordered me onto the coach. 'You're not welcome here,' he said. On the ferry back, everyone was barred from talking to me. I realised Gouldy was raging. When we got back he got stuck in. Not the usual dressing-down, but a warning that he'd had enough and wasn't going to defend me any more. The papers had a field day with the incident and Gouldy came out and announced, 'I'm banning Jones from the club, indefinitely.'

Sam Hammam paid me a home visit – the type he paid when things were going wrong. Gouldy banned me from playing in the Charity Shield at Wembley, Wimbledon against the champions, Liverpool, in a repeat of the match where we ruined their chances of doing the double. Gouldy refused to have me in the team. He stuck to the suspension. I don't believe Gouldy ever relented. I know for a fact Fash and Sam Hammam pleaded with him to have a think about it and do nothing rash. Looking back on it now, I also think Sam picked the team – I had my suspicions at the time, but now I know he was having an influence on the manager.

I knew I'd made mistakes but, having helped win the Cup, I resented what he was up to. However, as with most things, time healed the rift.

We lost the first game of the season and I thought, Right, Gouldy, you need me.

But one thing time will never heal was an incident just after I got going again, with Spurs' England international Gary Stevens.

We played at Tottenham and I was somewhere around the centre of the pitch when Fash had Stevens alongside him trying to nick possession. They seemed to be jockeying for ages, so I ran over. I was almost there when Stevens got the ball, but he was still half tangled up with Fash.

I went sliding in with a block tackle on the ball and went right through with it. It sent the two of them flying. Both of them were down receiving treatment. Fash got up. Stevens didn't. He tried to play on but his knee was all over the place and they took him off.

There was no way that I meant to 'do' Gary. I went in strong, as I usually do. I still believe Gary Stevens was the victim of one of those things that can just happen in football. There doesn't have to be malice behind serious injuries on the pitch.

I think he'd suffered a lot of knee trouble before and that one block tackle had finally been too much.

But I still had to be smuggled out from White Hart Lane in the back of Don Howe's car to avoid at least five hundred Spurs fans who had gathered outside like a furious picket-line mob gearing up for a fight.

Don Howe brought his car round and I got in and crouched on the floor. Don spread his coat on me and the supporters saw only him.

I told my new agent, Jerome Anderson, they were going to go for me but it had been an honest tackle. Some argued it was reckless, that there was no need for it. The next day I went to the hospital in London where Gary was lying. The woman on the desk rang up and then told me, 'He knows who you are and he doesn't want to see you. He won't let you go up.'

I thought he'd see in the cold light of day, from the tapes, there was nothing malicious in it. I'd picked up every sports magazine I could get my hands on and told the receptionist to make sure he got them.

I picked up the paper the next day to find they were all about Gary Stevens's career being in ruins because of a 'sick' Vinnie Jones tackle. I was accused of sending him a boxing magazine as a joke, but that really pissed me off. I sent every sports mag I could – it had nothing to do with a dig or a wind-up.

We met in Mauritius in the summer of 1997. We got talking quite a bit but that tackle still played on his mind. I really wish, 100 per cent, my tackle hadn't resulted in ending his run, but there's nothing I can do to change it. If I could take that tackle back now, with hindsight and everything, of course I would. What bothered me about the whole thing was that I tried to rectify it at the time and talk to the bloke and pacify the situation. It got to me that he went to the press about it with a story that just wasn't true – and then carried on for years telling that same story on the after-dinner circuit. I still stand by my theory that, if his knee had been sound, it would have withstood my move.

He couldn't accept it and his whingeing nearly got him a right-hander from Mick Harford, who was pissed off with him for keeping going on about it.

Just as I still can't accept what happened at Goodison Park in February 1989. I had already been cautioned for a foul on Peter Reid. Then I tackled Graeme Sharp, a tough Scottish international. My challenge was a stretching tackle. I reached too far, not trying to hurt him, but I caught him too late and on the top of his foot and he went over. Other players piled over and, as I jumped to my feet, Kevin Ratcliffe charged over and confronted me, face to face. So I stuck out my chest and put my head forward and, in the heat of the moment, snarled, 'Come on, then, if you want it.' I didn't thrust my head at him – I swear I was inches away and never made any contact. But he flew back as if I'd nutted him. If it had been a Sky broadcast now, with every blade of grass covered from every angle by cameras, then the footage would have disgraced him.

It was two cautions and I was off – no questions.

Don was livid. He screamed, 'What am I doing at this club with you? You're thugs, barbarians.' I didn't dare open my trap. I'd always respected Don.

But Gould was speechless in the dressing room. I protested my innocence but the headlines convicted me.

I went to see Sam Hammam at the end of the 1988–9 season because the publicity was making me a mental wreck. I'd been on the chat shows, *Wogan* and *The Jonathan Ross Show*, and it was the same old stuff: 'Why are you the hard man of football?' Then, at the end of the interviews, a red card. Stuff like that was beyond a joke to me.

Hard men, real nutcases, have something missing inside. And I don't regard myself in that bracket. I had lost it in some situations but in my heart I knew I was an honest lad. Not a 'dirty bastard'.

Sam and I talked for hours. I tried to persuade him to save me but he gave me a lot of reasons for saying no.

I complained, 'I have to wake up to the papers every day, the adverse publicity. The football doesn't get a mention.'

Sam was in tears by this point. So was I. I was in tears about leaving the Crazy Gang – the dream seemed to be over and a whirlwind spell with a bunch of lads I was really close to was coming to an end.

But the conversation reached a sort of friendly stalemate and as I went to leave he handed me my coat and said he'd think about it.

I'd made it as far as St John's Wood station, four or five minutes away, in my car when I got a call. It was Bill Fotherby, managing director of Leeds United.

It was over for me at Wimbledon. I was on my way to Leeds.

'We can meet with you today and Sam wants the deal done – and no agents, or press knowing,' Bill said.

I drove to the Oxford Street offices of Top Man, their sponsors, there and then.

I was on £500 a week at Wimbledon. When I walked in and saw Bill Fotherby, director Peter Ridsdale and Leeds's marketing man, Alan Roberts, standing with a bottle of champagne, they asked how much I wanted. I told them.

Bill stood up, spat on his palm, and said, 'Done. Here's my hand, it's a deal.' And we shook on it.

I was buzzing. The question of a car soon came up and I asked Peter Ridsdale if there was any chance of a BMW 325i. He agreed.

They also put me up in a suite at the Hilton Hotel, telling me

I'd be there until I found my own place. I had three months to get one.

My dad told me, 'This is big time, son. Big time.'

It's unsurprising that I soon became fond of the people at Leeds. And I realised everybody connected to the club, down to the tea ladies, was crackers about it.

It may have seemed big time, but there was rot in the team, a division between players who felt their days were numbered and new up-and-comers.

And I missed Fash terribly. I often wanted to ring Sam and beg to be taken back to Wimbledon.

But the Elland Road fans went bananas when I first ran on the pitch as a sub. It couldn't have gone better for me. I played a through ball from midfield, which was a bit heavy. It was going towards the Queens Park Rangers' keeper and it bobbled up, over his head and in! I went running straight to the Kop and that was it from there on in – I felt like a cult hero and I came to be idolised at Leeds, as the 1989–90 season turned out to be massive for the club. They were desperate to get out of the old Second Division and back among the big boys.

The Elland Road fans loved me and the feeling was mutual. People have always argued that I was most effective playing for teams fighting for their lives. But I didn't let my dog out trying to achieve it at Leeds.

In fifty-three appearances I was booked only twice – against Swindon at home in September 1989 and at Wolverhampton the following March. Both were cautions for minor fouls. And I scored five goals.

There was no tension at Leeds – and a complete trust in manager Howard Wilkinson. Howard Wilkinson was a doctor of football to me. He was a classy guy with a real air of authority. All of my managers, except Gouldy, had my complete respect – but Howard was really special. I call him Howard now because we spoke on the phone in early 2013 and he said, 'Don't call me Boss any more, son. Call me Howard.' That was a big moment. It was strange, when I heard that Fergie had said the same to his players after he left Manchester United in 2013. I couldn't help but think he got that from Howard. He was a man with the stature you would expect to manage a club like Leeds; he was perfect for us. He had a great combination of football knowledge, man-management skills and motivation.

I would look out on the pitch at Elland Road and see players like Dave Batty and Gordon Strachan doing some really skilful things and I felt so proud to be wearing the same shirt as they wore.

One of the reasons I got the cautions at Leeds was that I found the refereeing far less strict in the Second Division. But I was no longer the bull in the china shop. In many matches, I turned into a monster and forgot the football because I wanted to win at all costs.

But – and it may sound a bit odd – I never felt proud of my improved discipline. It was far from all trouble-free, though. I ended up having a proper scrap on the fire escape of a nightclub – Mr Craig's in Leeds city centre – and I was arrested. I'd been standing at the bar having a laugh when this bloke started mouthing off, obviously after trouble.

Wilkinson rang me and slaughtered me. Unfortunately, the fight coincided with a massive effort to clear bother from the notorious element of our own supporters

Wilkinson then summoned me to his office, saying, 'You've let me down, the players down, the fans – everybody.' A real man-to-man dressing-down.

But he didn't leave me out of the side. I wasn't charged. I was left with a few bruises for a few days.

The club had hit a bit of a dodgy spell late in the season after going ten points clear. Our luck had run out as well, and Sheffield United were catching us. We needed to win at Bournemouth in the last match to clinch the championship. It was a beautiful sunny day with thousands upon thousands of Leeds fans down there – about two thousand able to get into the ground and what seemed like another ten thousand outside.

Chris Kamara did the business down the right, crossed, and Lee Chapman scored. Leeds were champions and poor old Bournemouth were relegated.

For me, it was the nearest I'll ever get to the elation of winning that Cup final against Liverpool again. Coming home was brilliant. At a supermarket on the way back, we spent £50 on crates of beer and had a good drink along the way.

Howard Wilkinson – as usual – sat down the front sipping his Glenmorangie and smoking a big Havana. He did that every week on the way back home after a win.

It would have been 11 p.m. at least when we got back. All our cars were parked at Elland Road and the car park was full of fans' cars. The place was jumping. Dave Batty, the late Gary Speed – God rest his soul – and I jumped into a mate's car with the sunroof open and went into the city centre. Leeds was packed that night. You'd have thought we'd won the World Cup instead of the Second Division. Fans were everywhere, packing the pavements, clinging to statues and chasing the car with me Batty and Speedo standing, poking ourselves through the sunroof. We waved and clapped as loudly as the fans until a copper shouted for us to get back inside. We hit a club and word had got out that the whole team would be there, leading to a queue outside that stretched to the Yorkshire border.

They were fantastic memories – a great manager, great lads, great results. And great fun.

One night, I played a trick on Dave Batty because I knew he used to leave the back door to his house open. I stuck on a balaclava and shot round there at two in the morning. I grabbed a dustbin lid and snuck in to Batty and woke him up by clonking him gently on the head with the bin lid. He was on his feet in a split second, brandishing a bloody massive sheath knife he kept at his side. He realised it was me and I ran into the motor and tore off. I did a little handbrake turn at the bottom of the road, came back and drove straight over his lawn before tearing away up the road. We were all laughing at stuff like that at Leeds by the end of the season. Batty's lawn may still have been showing tyre marks but everything else was rosy. Or so I thought.

My heart sank at the start of the second season – and I gave both barrels on my way out of the club.

I'd returned after the summer to find the name of Gary McAllister by my peg in the first team dressing room. It was an absolute killer of a moment for me in football. The boss hadn't told

Man of the Match at Bushey International University, Watford – back in the days when I used to look to my granddad for guidance

We went up to Liverpool to play Burscough, a game organised by my dad's cousin. My dad was manager of Bedmond. 38-years-ago, in 1975, I would have been ten.

The house I bought in Shadwell when I went to Leeds United, posing with the sponsored car I got from the club.

One of many kisses from my proud nan, Annie Jones.

Just off the A3 at the Robin Hood roundabout – Richardson Evans Memorial Ground training with Fash. That was my first year at Wimbledon under Dave Bassett.

A few new faces brought in to Wimbledon FC by Bobby Gould after Dave Bassett had left.

Letting Gazza know I'm there. Plough Lane, SW19.

Terry Phelan and Dennis Wise, FA Cup Final. Winners against all the odds.

Having a laugh with the match-day mascot in front of the Kop at Elland Road.

My old drinking buddy Elton John at Vicarage Road. Both of us lifelong Watford supporters.

Tan and I had just bought the farm at Redbourne where we were to be married. Our first home together.

Signing the wedding registry in Watford with Tans, the day before the 'big' day.

With Kaley at the first house we had in LA. Bill Withers' place, next door to Pete Sampras.

A proud moment – Aaron joining the army. Here he is in his first year.

Lock Stock – Big Chris in action.

Sharing a laugh on the set of Lock Stock, watching the playback.

At the Savoy Hotel being congratulated by one of my idols, Sir Michael Caine, after I won Best British Actor at the Evening Standard Film Awards in 1998.

The premiere of *Lock Stock and Two Smoking Barrels* and my first ever as the star of a film. The repair bills were more than the hotel bills after that night out.

Me and my old mucker Sting enjoy a chat at the Four Seasons in Beverly Hills.

With the late Dennis Farina, who I became very close friends with, shooting *Snatch*.

Another premiere, this time for *Snatch* in London, all the boys having the craic after the fantastic reception we got.

me – that was just the first part of my finding out. But I worked just as hard in training. Howard Wilkinson kept us guessing with his plans for the new season. He would mix the midfield up: some days we would play in a three in training, with me and McAllister in there; other days it would be a four without me. It was a tough time, but he had us all battling for our place in the starting XI. In our first game preseason we were flying after twenty minutes. We had created loads of chances with a midfield three with me, Batty and McAllister. I can't help wondering what would have happened if we had scored in those twenty minutes. Would he have kept me on? That's football – we will never know. That was just how the cards fell for me at the time.

I was carrying my pride at helping the club to the Second Division championship – a £60 tattoo. It neatly balanced the Wimbledon tattoo on the outside of the other leg: 'FA Cup winners, 1988'.

But the graft in training didn't seem to make a dent. Wilkinson shot me down. He didn't even have me in the list of substitutes when the first line-up was announced. That really broke my heart.

I was in one of the sponsors' suites when someone wandered up to me and said, 'I can't believe you're not even a sub considering everything you've done for this club.' I welled up. I had to get out quickly or I'd have broken down. My mind was confused. Part bewilderment, part anger. I couldn't work out what was going on. But it didn't take a genius to work out that my days at Leeds were numbered. I had that terrible feeling of rejection again and I felt desperate.

I longed for somebody like Gordon Strachan to speak up, to

say to the boss, 'Vinnie's flying in training but he's not even a sub. What are you doing?'

I wanted to have my say, but I had so much respect for the gaffer, I bit my tongue and thought my hard work would do the talking. But eventually I cracked.

Around the fifth game of the season, away to Luton, I still hoped to be back in the side. I'd been doing some shooting up in Leeds and was planning to take my kit on the coach because I was due to stay the weekend in Watford. Everybody was on the coach before me and, as Wilkinson went to get on board, I said something sarcastic like 'Will I be needing my boots today?' He wasn't amused.

Then when I opened the boot of my car, the idea struck: the shotgun!

I took it out from its sleeve and, as the players looked out from the coach, I saw their expressions change and everybody turned deadly silent.

As I stepped inside the coach Wilkinson looked up, I put the end of the twelve-bore right up his nostrils with my finger on the trigger and said, 'Now, are you going to bloody play me at Luton tomorrow?'

I kept a straight face long enough for him to seriously wonder. Of course, the gun wasn't loaded and the safety mechanism was clicked in place. But for a second or two he looked seriously worried.

Then, as I replaced a scowl with a smile and then a laugh, Wilkinson cracked up. He was the first to appreciate the gag and the laughter tore through the entire coach – Howard appreciated it more than anybody.

The real laugh was that he did play me at Luton.

Once the team had been named I went to pick my usual shirt, No. 4. I was told, 'Er, Vin, you're not number four today. Batty's got four.'

'You're joking,' I said. 'I've worn the four shirt all my life, even as a kid. I'm not stopping now.'

Wilkinson told me: 'You wear the number eight, and Batty wears number four.'

I was gutted. And it wasn't made much better when I was brought off in the second half. The writing was on the wall for me at this point. His mind was made up.

I trained like a Trojan again the week after but Wilkinson took me aside and told me he'd had Dave Bassett on the phone. Bassett was manager of United now, having left Watford in 1988. I was speechless. It was like telling the Queen she was on her way out of Buckingham Palace. I'd been at my happiest at Leeds, playing proper football and loving the whole professional feel of the place. Leeds and I had connected really well. Around town I felt welcome and I had become a big part of the community, with the restaurants and bars treating me like royalty with doors open wherever I went. They even gave me my own radio show on Radio Air on a Friday night from 6 to 7 p.m. I would speak to fans and interview my teammates. I loved it – and it was a little taste of what was to come.

But now this.

My immediate reaction was 'Right, bollocks. I'll go.'

That evening I met Sheffield United's assistant manager, Geoff Taylor. He took me to Bassett's house – virtually right next door to Wilkinson's. I'd already made up my mind. It doesn't matter what you've done for a club, how much you feel about them – you're on your own in these circumstances.

I tried to keep a level head about the situation, but it was no good. The bull had been let loose in the china shop again. The dog had bolted out of the cage. I phoned my dad and he was dead against it: 'Sleep on it, son, sleep on it. Do you realise where Sheffield United are?' I did. At the bottom of the First Division.

Dad used to come to all the Leeds games and was aware of my popularity up there.

But I agreed to join Harry Bassett that night. Sheffield were paying Leeds £700,000 which was more than I was getting at Elland Road.

Sheffield United had got off to a rotten start that season. Bassett wanted me in as captain but Dad still insisted, 'You'll always regret it.'

In footballing terms, I was going backwards. It was 'hump and run' football. By now Bassett was a percentages man. He would have a guy in the stands counting pass completion rates, percentages of corners with shots on targets and all sorts. Leeds was different – Bassett played decent football at times, but it still felt like a step back from that great Leeds team. And Sheffield United weren't as good as the Wimbledon side I'd left.

My start to the season at Sheffield's Bramall Lane was depressing. We lost a lot of games and I was being made man of the match on a regular basis for just giving it 100%. I was back to the brawn and aggression and the bookings were flying left, right and centre. There were spells when the players didn't dare to go near town because of the backlash from fans.

Sheffield United were really struggling to make an impression in the old First Division and Bassett was getting increasingly worried. He had brought me in as a leader and eventually asked me what I thought we could do – because, if we didn't do something, we'd be going down. We talked for a while and then he said, 'Go and tell the boys I'll put a hundred grand in the players' pool if we stay up.' Maybe it was coincidence that we went on to win seven matches on the trot, which took us up to twelfth, so we survived. I think we had seven points at Christmas.

It wasn't without controversy, of course, and another unwelcome record for me: booked after five seconds of a match against Manchester City at Maine Road. Those brilliant days, the concentration on passing the ball at Leeds, were well and truly dead. My mood wasn't right, I was feeling so low. My head was down because I had thrived under Wilkinson with guys like Gordon Strachan around me. Now it was route one all over again. I found myself back in my bashing days.

But I wasn't totally miserable all the time at Sheffield. I rented a cottage close to a golf course and I had started seeing my old flame. We had first met in a nightclub where she was working at the time.

But we'd grown apart in my time at Leeds. She had a very good job as a PA to the governor of a bank, and so we saw less and less of each other. But, after the move to Sheffield, I started going back to Watford more, and we'd link up at the cottage.

What came next didn't come as a complete shock when she said, 'I've something to tell you. I'm pregnant.'

I didn't go all gooey and silly, just said, 'Phew!' I was well pleased. Really, I was over the moon.

Everyone was telling me during her pregnancy, 'This is what

you need. This will settle you down. This is the best thing for you.'

Not in my case.

Some blokes change their characters, but I just go with the flow.

At the close of season, we had been at her house and were on the way back to Sheffield when she started to suffer what I thought were stomach cramps. 'I'll be all right,' she said. So we kept driving up the M1. After all, it was six weeks before the baby was due.

We carried on until somewhere around Leicester Forest East services, where her waters broke. I didn't know what that was all about but was put into a panic when I phoned the hospital in Sheffield and they told me, 'Bring her straight here.'

Tests confirmed the baby was on its way and not much of an examination was needed before getting her into the operating theatre quickly. I went in as well and was really frightened for her because of the pain she was going through.

But after not too long the baby was out – a boy. The nurse passed him to me – they hadn't severed the cord. I was just motionless. They smacked his bum, put a tube in his mouth and then I was able to hold him for a minute. I didn't say a word. I was completely speechless but felt ten feet tall – until the doctor told me to hand him back and my legs started to shake, out of control.

It was the doc's routine to go into the pub next door to the hospital following births during opening hours. He said to me, 'Come on, let's go and wet the baby's head while these people tidy things up.' I gave my boy's mum a kiss and I kissed the baby and within a few minutes of the birth I found myself in the pub. All the locals knew the doctor and knew the score – brilliant. I wanted to ask him about babies. He wanted to ask about football.

We called our baby Aaron and went mental at Mothercare buying every toy and item of clothing available. Being premature, Aaron needed special care at first and I was desperate when they told me he had jaundice. I was soon reassured when I was told it was normal in the circumstances.

Aaron's arrival thrilled me to bits, and, now he's in his twenties, I'm just as proud. I went out with a couple of the players and got drunk out of my mind. I was so proud.

We were both overjoyed at Aaron's arrival but I hadn't expected the difficulties we would face. Aaron was six weeks premature and had had two weeks in an incubator. He'd suffered from severe jaundice, but came through unscathed. A lot of people, including my dad, said that having a child would change me. I was wandering through life waiting for this moment to change me after Aaron was born, but it never happened. I was exactly the same and it never really felt any different. But our situation began to change, which was no one's fault. But the overall circumstances were bad: a couple under pressure, a baby crying and a professional footballer worried about the lack of sleep. We tiptoed around each other.

It was obvious to me we were growing apart. In an attempt to sort out the future, I suggested we buy a house, and we moved in together. But drastic change wasn't far away.

Sheffield United had played at Coventry early in 1991–2. On a day off, Dave Bassett rang me.

'Jonah, how are you? Listen, I've agreed a fee with Chelsea for you,' he said.

Relief washed over me. Relieved to be away from the crash-bang game I'd returned to at Sheffield. Excited at the prospect of joining the likes of Wisey again and Andy Townsend at Stamford Bridge.

So, instead of having the day off, I went and signed for Chelsea within an hour. Another fee of £575,000.

I had played against Andy Townsend and rated him highly as a player. Wisey and I nicknamed him 'the Beak' because of his massive conk. He was a busy bloke as a player, always talking and getting involved in everything. It was the Beak and Wisey who told Chelsea's manager Ian Porterfield to sign me, and that was what happened. My debut was a dream, we won 4–1 against Luton Town. I ran straight up to the fans and started singing, 'One man went to mow . . .' That was it – they were on my side! I got a shock because it was the first time I had seen real player power. Porterfield would have meetings in the car park after we had played and lost. He would ask us where we thought it was going wrong and what he should do, which was sad, really. That was *his* job, and he should have known what was going on and run things more professionally.

The boys were telling me recently that Andy had changed his mobile number – he has moved on to being the big TV hotshot now; things have moved on. I can't watch him do punditry: it just makes me crease up listening to the Beak rattle on, being all sensible!

Not long after I'd signed for Chelsea – would you believe it? – we were back at Sheffield United.

Aaron's mum and I saw less and less of each other and I moved into Hunters Oak, Hemel Hempstead, with my football pal Joe Allon, the centre-forward Chelsea had signed from Hartlepool at the time.

Joe and I treated the place like a bachelor pad – nights out, women, booze, fast cars, training and playing football. Good times – on full blast.

As usual, it wasn't all laughs. There was nothing funny about the night we came out of a club and stood by a taxi rank. A couple of blokes were waiting for a cab and minding their own business until one of them started to have a go at Joe.

They said, 'What are you looking at?' Then one of them turned nasty. 'Listen, mate,' I said. 'If you want to get to him, you'll have to go through me first.' And he did. Or at least he tried to, and the two of us ended up in a real street fight.

I finished with a big gash in my left ear and a split head that was going to need stitches. In the end, we both stood up, both completely knackered, looked each other in the eyes and shook hands. Then, when the first cab pulled up, he said, 'Go on, pal, you have it.' When I got in he added, 'And good luck on Saturday.' Bloody funny when you think about it.

At the training ground afterwards, there were reporters everywhere. Someone from that cab rank had tipped them off. Bob Ward, the physio, was stitching my head when, as luck would have it, the chairman Ken Bates wandered in. 'What the fuck have you been doing?' he asked. 'I came second last night, Batesy,' I said. He muttered something before leaving. I could tell he wasn't amused.

I was enjoying being at Chelsea, so I didn't want to upset anybody. I got a strange kind of aura back, though, and started strutting around with a chest like a cock pigeon.

A few feathers were being ruffled – especially when I beat that record five-second booking.

The FA Cup brought Sheffield United to the Bridge and you're always wound up a bit tighter playing against a former club. But my first move, my first challenge, brought the yellow card from ref Keith Burge's pocket. I was straight in on Dane Whitehouse. I must have been too high, too wild, too strong or too early because, after three seconds, I could hardly have been too bloody late.

I also picked up a ridiculous £1,500 fine by the FA for making 'obscene gestures' at fans before our match against Arsenal at Highbury. I'd seen my sister's boyfriend Tony O'Mahoney in the crowd and had mouthed, 'You wanker' while making the classic gesture. The FA stuck me with a penalty, but the truth never came out. What a joke.

I had a great craic with the Chelsea boys. But it had turned out to be a bit of a holiday camp. At the end of the season I told them they needed to bring someone like my old coach Don Howe in. He was brilliant at Wimbledon and he would bring some order to the place. Our boss, the late Ian Porterfield (he died in 2007), was a big drinker. He was a lovely bloke, but he wasn't really managing the team – the players were a bit strong for him. Training was pretty shambolic: just lads playing five-a-side, or assistant manager Stan Ternent would turn up and ask the boys what they wanted to do today.

We were only a few games into the 1992–3 season when the wheel turned full circle. I was on the golf course and a waiter kept running out to me to tell me that there was someone from

Chelsea on the phone. I knew instinctively that my time was up. I went in and took the call from Managing Director Colin Hutchinson. He offered me a certain amount to leave, and I said no. I went back out to the golf course, and the waiter came running out again. I told him to say no and then the price went up £10,000 every time the waiter came out again!

I was on the move again – back to Wimbledon. Here I come again, for £640,000 or thereabouts. I was gutted that Chelsea were moving me out. I heard a story – and I don't know how true it was – that their goalkeeping coach Eddie Niedzwiecki was big mates with Nigel Spackman and maybe he wanted him back at Chelsea.

I'm not annoyed at him. What got up my nose was Chelsea thinking they could replace me with Spackman, who I thought couldn't lace my boots at the time.

But he came in from Glasgow Rangers and I was off to Wimbledon.

I had recently fallen out with my agent, Jerome Anderson, after I got in massive hassle for appearing in that notorious *Soccer's Hard Men* video and took up with Steve Davies (who is no longer with us). We developed into great friends. I didn't want any troubles any more and it was on Steve's advice that I invested in a promotions company and IT firm.

Back at Wimbledon, in the glittering Premier League, I had a great welcome on my home debut. My photograph was all over the front of the match programme and in it I told fans they would be seeing a different Vinnie Jones – 'One who can pass the ball, not just hook it on aimlessly. It won't just be crash, bang, wallop.'

So what happens? Typical bloody mayhem.

It was against Kenny Dalglish's Blackburn, the moneybags brigade. I lasted about thirty minutes before the referee sent me packing. Two of Blackburn's players, Tony Dobson and Mike Newell, were to be dismissed later on. But you don't need telling whose name dominated the headlines. I started by passing the ball, but it was when I didn't have it that trouble could start. Kevin Moran, Blackburn's Irish international defender, had it and I challenged him from behind. He later described it to the press by saying I'd hooked him with my arms round his neck in a tackle 'more like rugby than football'.

Referee Martin Bodenham immediately followed his yellow card for the challenge with a red when I swore at Moran. John Fashanu weighed in, protesting the decision, and he had to be dragged away.

I spent the rest of the match watching from Sam Hammam's private box at Selhurst Park, Plough Lane having been sold off. And I was blazing. I was convinced my reputation, as much as my behaviour, was going to land me back in trouble at Wimbledon. After all, I hadn't been sent off at Leeds or Chelsea.

Manager Joe Kinnear went on the record after, saying, 'Vinnie gets mistreated. There is abusive language from nearly every player, nearly every week. Referees could send them all off. It's crazy. Vinnie is like a marked man.' What a difference it was to hear that from your manager. Bobby Gould would have thrown me to the wolves, I suspected.

That November, I was hauled before the FA disciplinary officials for the *Soccer's Hard Men* video I appeared in. I'd agreed to take part after my old agent Jerome Anderson had phoned and said there was two grand on the table for taking part in a movie about ... soccer's hard men. I kick myself for being so naïve. I never had a copy, I hadn't even watched it and wouldn't want one in my home.

I told the FA people I'd been stupid and that I totally dissociated myself from glamorising violence on the pitch. 'Don't condemn me for one bad mistake,' I said. But I was slapped with a record £20,000 fine, plus a six-month ban, suspended for three years. I've been made to pay for that mistake – and others.

Over the years I've watched other players receiving punishments for incidents in the game. Only Eric Cantona's stands out as a similar punishment. With both of us, there was a case of reputation playing a part in the decisions.

By this time in my football career, the mud had stuck. I was seen as a hard man first and a footballer second – it wouldn't be until the late nineties that that reputation would pay any dividends.

8

Tanya

It was my Chelsea mate Joe Allon who spotted the beginning of the rest of my life. It was a lovely day and Joe was lounging by the window of our gaff in Hunters Oak, Hemel Hempstead. He glanced out into the street and said, 'God, what a stunner! Come and have a look at this.'

He wasn't exaggerating. I saw a gorgeous woman walking by. Then I did a double-take.

'It's Tanya,' I told him. 'I know her.'

'Course you do,' he said, with all the sarcasm you'd expect.

But it was her. It was Tanya. The first time I'd seen her in years. And I sat and told Joe how it had all started . . .

Tanya was among the kids who used to go to the Sunday cricket matches. I went with the family of another pal. We were just kids, about twelve. There was nothing boy–girl about it when I was hanging about with Tanya and her pal.

Tans went to Langleybury and we lost touch.

I didn't see her for years until, one night, this girl came up to me in the Three Horseshoes pub in Watfordand said, 'You're Vincent Jones, aren't you?'

I had to do a double-take back then, too, before I realised it was Tanya. She was beautiful – I recognised that all right. Gorgeous, with long, dark hair. The other lads knew who she was. When it dawned on me, we stood and chatted about those cricket matches all those years before.

She said her dad would never let her go to the pub but her mum had agreed on condition she get back before her dad. I saw her in there a couple of times again and one night I decided to ask if I could walk her home.

I had taken my motorbike to the pub, so I left it outside as Tanya and I wandered back into her street. It ended in nothing romantic – a cup of tea in the kitchen with her mum, Maureen.

When I walked back to the pub, I realised there was no bloody motorbike. I wandered round clutching the great big helmet the thieves had left behind.

I went over to a phone box and heard a bike roaring up and down the park just as I was dialling for a lift from a pal. I walked over and there was a crowd of lads taking it in turns to ride – on *my* bike.

Time for action.

I positioned myself behind a tree to meet the rider and as he ripped towards me, I caught him with a right-hander. Off he came, over went the bike and I was on it and away like a shot before his mates could catch up with me.

When I saw Tanya in the pub the week after, I accused her of setting me up. She said she had nothing to do with it. We also had a falling-out because a mate of mine had told her I'd said I'd kissed her in her house after I walked her home. 'What's this about you telling your friend you got off with me in my mum's house?' she said. There hadn't even been a hug, and I think Russell was a bit jealous I'd walked her home, so had pulled her leg. She didn't see the funny side – and that was it. She blew me out completely and I was upset.

I tried to creep back in but she was having none of it. She kept giving me the cold shoulder and that was that.

We didn't set eyes on one another again until 1984.

It was FA Cup final day – Watford against Everton. As I went to park the car, the coach carrying the Watford players' wives and girlfriends breezed past. Yet another double-take – Tanya was on there. She was pointing me out to Suzy Barnes, John Barnes's wife. She must have wondered why Tanya was highlighting a bloke on the dole – this was long before I was playing at Wealdstone or going to Sweden. I found out later that, when Tanya was telling Suzy, 'That's Vincent Jones,' she just said, 'Who's that?'

Tanya was going out with Steve Terry, Watford's centre-half'.

I watched her walking up the Wembley steps to see Steve play. She was the most beautiful person I'd ever seen.

A couple of years later, I saw a piece in the *Watford Evening Echo* about how Tanya had undergone heart-transplant surgery at Harefield Hospital after complications giving birth to Kaley. I read with mixed emotions: sad for her suffering and relieved she'd recovered.

It was part of another of those strange coincidences in my life – unless Granddad had something to do with it.

Tanya was actually living next door but one to me in Hunters Oak and I'd had no idea. I'd seen her pass by in a car and I'd also noticed Steve going in and out. It all fell into place when I bumped into Tanya's friend Joanne Southern. She explained how she and Tanya were living at the house together because Tanya and Steve had split and were going through a divorce.

I couldn't work out how to approach her. In the end, Kaley's rabbit did the trick. Joe had told me he'd taken it off the road one day and given it back to Tanya – she'd told him he was always escaping.

I decided to use that snippet of information to get my foot in the door. I went round after an evening in the pub and knocked on Tanya's door. I told her that the rabbit George had been out again and I'd gone to her garage to put him back in his hutch. Then Kaley, about four at the time, started crying. 'Excuse me, I've got to go upstairs for my little girl,' Tanya said.

I was a bit merry at that stage and not lacking in confidence.

I walked in while Tanya was upstairs, put the kettle on, made some coffee, found the biscuits in the drawer and took the lot into the living room. When Tanya came down she thought I'd gone. 'In here,' I said. 'It was freezing so I came in and put the kettle on.' She was being all prim and proper. 'Do you always walk into people's houses and put the kettle on?' she asked.

But we had the coffee and biscuits and we sat talking for hours and hours. I got the old Hamlet cigar going and we kept talking. Tanya asked things like how I got into football and told me she couldn't believe I'd become a player because she always thought I would end up in jail somewhere.

We talked about how she and Steve had grown apart and about babies. But she didn't say anything about the heart transplant.

I didn't leave until seven the next morning, when Kaley woke up. I went home, drove in for training and was back at her house again that afternoon. It was hot and we sat out the back with our friends.

At weekends, a crowd of girls gathered at the house and I often went round there to sit in the sunshine, chatting and having a great time. Things just progressed and we started going out as a crowd.

Tanya and I were getting to know each other, growing together, becoming closer – but not even holding hands, let alone sealing things with a kiss.

There came a day when she said she had to go away for the weekend, to hospital in Nuneaton for laser treatment to sort some women's problems – nothing to do with her heart but serious all the same. Her mum was going up to visit and she'd be there for a few days to rest. The thought of her in that hospital drove me mad, so I asked if I could go with her.

I drove up to Nuneaton and, as usual – whatever state she might be in – Tans made sure she looked nice. She'd already been at the mascara and lip gloss before she knew I would be there.

After a while at her bedside with her mum, we were left alone together. I held Tanya's hands and gave her a little kiss. Just a gentle, little one. It was the very first time I kissed her. I'd already made up my mind that I was in love with her. That was why I had to drive to that hospital. I had never felt that way about a girl before. I knew I wanted to take care of her.

While she was in hospital, I went to check in on her house. I came across a pile of letters almost as thick as a phone directory. They were bills, many of them of the red variety. I suppose she couldn't cope with them at the time, so I sat down and wrote cheques to clear the lot.

After I'd put my hands on hers and given her that little kiss, that was us. When I went back to the hospital she looked me in the eye and said, 'Vin, you've got to take me home. Please get the doctor to let me go.' I asked but the doctor said something that amounted to, 'You've got to be joking.'

But Tanya was begging. I picked her up and carried her down the corridors of that hospital and out to the car. It was like the last scene in *An Officer and a Gentleman*, one of our favourite films, with all the nurses applauding us as we left. I loaded her in the back still in her pyjamas and covered her up with blankets. The car was filled with flowers from her bedside and that was the way I drove her home.

Tanya was still recovering when we had our first proper date – the wedding of a daughter of a good mate of mine, Johnny Watts. It was a top wedding and the bride and groom were whisked away by helicopter from the huge marquee. Tanya and I were still watching it fly off until it became just a dot in the sky, and when we looked around all the other guests had cleared off.

I said, 'That's going to be us on our wedding day.'

We held each other for ages, then drove back to Hunters Oak in Johnny's white Rolls-Royce. He'd insisted and we'd jumped at the chance, parking it in the driveway.

I started spending more and more time with Tanya and Kaley and the feeling grew that I wanted to take care of them for the rest of their lives. I wanted to make sure that no harm could ever come to them and it was inevitable that I would ask Tanya to marry me. It was quite a formal proposal.

We had just returned from a night out when I held her and calmly asked, 'Will you marry me? I want to marry you.'

'Yes,' she said. Actually, it was more of a shriek, and she went crazy about it.

I asked her not to tell anybody before I had asked her dad – I wanted to do it properly.

When I rang her dad Lou and asked if I could come round, he thought there was something wrong. He was alone when I arrived and I just said straight out, 'I wanted to ask you if I could marry Tans. I wanted to ask you for your blessing.'

Lou talked quietly and kindly about Tanya's heart transplant and he said, 'Do you know what you're taking on board? She's no ordinary girl and sometimes we have panic attacks about it all.'

I jumped in: 'I know all that and I want to look after her for the rest of her life.'

'Then I'm over the moon for you,' Lou said, giving me a big hug. He had never forgotten I was there to bring her home early from hospital in Nuneaton.

Before meeting Lou, I had phoned my dad, told him the news and asked him to find me a plot of land. He got me a spot in Redbourn. It was a derelict shell of a bungalow on three acres. We called it Oaklands – and from the front it is an exact replica of Woodlands, the bungalow Dad had bought for the family and done up.

I don't know whether I was trying to recreate that family home, but I even used the same architect, Ken Phillips, that my dad had used all those years ago.

We'd set a date for the wedding while I mucked in with the demolition and groundwork – 25 June 1994.

My stag night was something else. I went with my pals to Cork for the weekend – sixty-two of us, including Dad and Lou. There was lots of drinking and poker being played.

I knew the type of wedding I wanted – just like the one Johnny Watts had put on for his daughter. We had vast marquees, silver service, the finest food and a helicopter. First we went through a register-office ceremony on the Friday. Steve had sold the wedding to *News of the World* and the place was swarming with press, but the paper had left nothing to chance, surrounding the place with cardboard shields.

Johnny Moore was my best man – Johnny and his family had rescued me from misery when I was working and living in Reading. He took me back to his house, had a family meeting, and they decided I was to move back in. He got me back into football again, and for that I owe him everything. His business got into trouble years later and I lent him the money to see him through with the mortgage, which was a way of repaying him for what he had done for me. When he was back on his feet, he was straight round to pay me off.

My sister Ann was one of the bridesmaids, along with Kaley, and Aaron was a pageboy. There were four hundred guests – the Bedmond boys were all there with Dennis Wise, John Barnes and Sam Hammam.

It was a blazing hot day. Tanya didn't show it but she was in terrible pain from one of her feet – a temporary side effect from the drugs she has to take for her heart. She told me later she could hardly walk due to gout, but no one would ever have known.

One of the most moving moments was when Violet Brown sang after it was announced that we were dedicating the wedding to the memory of an old mate, Joe Byrne. She had sung at his funeral, which happened before the wedding. He was hit and killed by a car while finding his way home from a pub one night. When Violet sang 'Danny Boy' at his funeral, I decided I wanted to hear her at my wedding.

A hell of a lot of tears were shed at that ceremony – a lot of them mine and Tanya's.

The service flew by and a jazz band played right through the meal until more guests arrived for the black-tie disco afterwards. I sang to Tans during our dance a line from 'Where Do You Go To My Lovely?': 'When you go on your summer vacation, you go to Juan les Pins.' That was exactly where we went on our honeymoon.

When we came back, our housekeeper ran out to greet us and the garage doors went up – all our family and friends were there, for more drink and a fantastic buffet. I had a cuddle with Nana and said, 'It's a pity Granddad isn't here.'

'Oh, he is Vinnie, he is,' she said.

I look back on my mum and dad breaking up all those years ago, and now I have a real glow about us all being able to be close. I gave Mum away at her wedding to Dave Hockney and to see both sets of parents together for my wedding was wonderful.

9

Full-Time Whistle

On the pitch, things did not give me quite the same glow as Tanya, Aaron and Kaley. Nineteen ninety-four became an extraordinary year of ups and downs, but life rumbled on during my second spell at Wimbledon. I hit it off with Joe Kinnear, and loved the responsibility of being captain – and I had the respect of the players. But there was another sending-off at home to Leicester following a fistfight between me and David Lowe. Walking down the tunnel, I thought, Here we go again.

It happened again two months later. My tackle on Newcastle's Rob Lee must have looked horrendous – like a kung-fu kick, because I went straight in. Referee Philip Don just said as he sent me packing, 'Why have you made me do this?' I agreed.

The Crazy Gang element was still alive but not on the scale of the early days. Back then, cars would be smeared in Vaseline, car tyres let down, potatoes wedged up exhaust pipes. Frenchy the physio, who is another lifelong friend, was dangled over the edge of a boat on the way to a preseason trip in Scandinavia – all he was worried about was the change falling out of his pockets! The tricks on my return to the Dons weren't as extreme, but were still there. New arrivals this time round had their bootlaces cut and dodgy clothes removed and burned, and they were rugby-tackled, stripped and flung into a patch of nettles and into a river.

And, in December 1994, they had a new international in their ranks: Vincent Peter Jones of Wales! A possibility that I might qualify for the Republic of Ireland when Big Jack Charlton was on the lookout had fizzled out. And, again, the Wales move had something to do with Granddad. Arthur Jones's birth certificate was tracked down in time for me to join the Wales squad for the European Championship qualifying game against Bulgaria in Cardiff.

I blasted out 'Land of My Fathers' down the phone to my agent back then, when I drove over the Severn Bridge when everything was sorted.

I didn't ask Granddad for help before that first game for Wales: because he was a Welshman, his main passion was rugby.

It was great to hear that first whistle: it signalled my start as an international player. I know people laugh that I'm as Welsh as a rarebit, but I *feel* Welsh. And I'd brought up my ghetto blaster to Cardiff, belting out the Welsh national anthem on it every chance I got and singing along with it. Most of the players yelled at me to pack it in, but Gary Speed was one of the lads who sang along with me.

I was shocked to the core when I heard about Gary's death in

2011. It was so sad to hear how such a committed family man had decided to end it all. But, as you'll read later in this chapter, I have considered taking on my own demons in the same way.

Anyway, the massive honour of being able to play for Wales has overwhelmed details of the match. I did OK. I know that I enjoyed it, wearing that red shirt with the three feathers. At the time, I hadn't known many prouder moments in my life. Pride definitely came before a fall in my case.

The next match was a night game in June 1995, another European Championship qualifier, this time against Georgia. The match was won by Georgi Kinkladze with a glorious chip from twenty-five yards with about twenty minutes to go. Sadly, I wasn't on the pitch to see it – I had been sent packing after twenty-five minutes. Bobby Gould always said the most dangerous time for me as a player was when everything was going well – I would just knacker it up for myself. I had made a strong start in the game, winning all my headers and tackles, making accurate passes. I made a great block tackle and my tail was up. I was enjoying it.

Then it all kicked off.

I clattered into Mikhail Kavelashvili, who went down, and I trampled all over him. I couldn't argue about being sent off, but he made the most of it. I should have jumped out of the way, but he just rolled and rolled and rolled – made a real meal of it. As soon as I was red-carded, he was up on his feet again, running about as if nothing had happened.

That was my worst sending-off. Wales were like an early-days Wimbledon: they were striving for greater things and had a strong team spirit. I walked off the pitch and nobody came over to put an arm around me. I was in the wrong. When everyone came in at half-time I might as well have been something the dog left in the middle of the floor. To lose 1–0 with only ten men, that made it all the worse – I had let everyone down again.

I redeemed myself with some strong performances – but nothing memorable enough to mark me down as a Wales legend. In the meantime, Bobby Gould became the Wales manager. I feared my days were numbered. Yet he gave me the opportunity few footballers get: to lead out an international team as captain!

It was in Holland and the usual skipper Barry Horne was out injured. At the hotel the night before the game, Gouldy told the lads to write on a bit of paper the name of the player they wanted to see as skipper. Then the slips were read out – 'Vinnie Jones, Vinnie Jones . . .' I was voted captain of Wales by the lads.

Welsh recognition warranted another tattoo. And I had a beauty done – the dragon and feathers.

But, after nine caps, my international career was over. Bobby Gould's plans didn't include me. The first I knew about it was when the papers got in touch. But I never got a call from him about it. I read it on Ceefax. I still think he should have given me a ring.

Captaining the side for one game was enough for me, and I'll cherish that for ever, especially as it was against Holland, one of the best footballing sides in the world, with a team packed full of great players.

The 15th of February 1995 was a black day for me for two reasons. The international match between Terry Venables's England and Jack Charlton's Republic of Ireland had to be abandoned after twenty-seven minutes because of rioting by visiting England fans.

It was also the night that took me very close to suicide.

I'd been sent over to Dublin to write a piece for my column in a national newspaper. We were staying at Jurys Inn hotel and an incident at breakfast when I saw Gary Lineker set the tone.

This was the bloke who'd said Wimbledon should be watched only on Ceefax. I shouted across to him, 'Big ears, you're a disgrace. 'Not so big now, are you, big ears? Not as brave as when you're sitting talking on the telly?'

Then, I chucked a bit of toast at him and shouted, 'Put that behind your ear!' I asked him to say to my face what had got up his nose so much about Wimbledon.

When we heard the England-vs-Ireland match had been aborted, we stayed in the hotel drinking. I was sitting having a bottle of champagne with a few others, I spotted Ted Oliver, a news reporter from the *Daily Mirror*. Oliver said something innocuous but it led to a bit of grabbing and tugging. I got his head in my arm and took hold of his nose with my teeth. I thought it was totally in jest. Perhaps I got carried away with the drink in me. He told me to clear off but next minute someone runs over to me and shouts, 'You've bitten his nose.'

I went over to apologise but he had a handkerchief pressed over his nose and told me to clear off. I wasn't getting anywhere, so turned in.

The next morning I was on a flight back from Dublin with my mate Jim Creed, feeling good that I'd equalled the score with

Lineker. But at Stansted airport I walked into chaos. Somebody yelled, 'You bit off a bloke's nose in Ireland!' The story was that I'd amputated his hooter. I was straight on the phone to Tanya and she was crying. There were cameras and reporters at my house and radio and TV folk constantly on the phone.

I got home, gave Tanya a cuddle. I went upstairs and lay on the bed. I couldn't cope with everything that was happening around me. It wasn't a nervous breakdown, as such, but it was some sort of emotional collapse. I just lay there, my mouth open, staring into space. I couldn't move. It really was one of my darkest hours.

I had always faced and handled everything before. This time, I couldn't. There was me thinking what had happened in Ireland was a bit of horseplay and it had turned into a nightmare. The *Mirror* had it splashed over their front page the next day: 'Mirrorman's soccer riot agony', with a picture of Oliver and his damaged nose. Inside there were more pictures and the heading, 'Vinnie fixed me with his teeth and shook me like a dog with a dead rabbit'.

I didn't expect it. The editor was going to sack me from my column. In the end, they settled on the idea of my writing my side of the story.

I began to feel sick. I went back to lying in my curled-up position and the pressure squeezed and squeezed. I couldn't see a way out. Desperate times called for desperate measures – and I wasn't thinking rationally.

I looked at Tans and thought, She's found herself married to a monster – I *am* a monster.

There are some who think I'm a stupid, violent thug. At that moment in time, I felt like the monster some people had portrayed me as. The dog could not have strayed further from the kennel that night and I knew I was going to punish the pair of us.

I had made my mind up about what I was going to do. I had managed to soldier on through adversity up until this point, but it had gone too far this time.

First I wanted to say goodbye to Tans. Before she left to go shopping, I held her and kissed her, so as not to raise her suspicions in any way. I then took my gun and walked to the wood at the back of the house. It was dark, bitterly cold and spitting rain. I knew exactly where I wanted to do it: a little corner where bluebells grew in spring. I had my own little seat there, an old oil drum, and I knew it would be there.

I sat on the drum, put the gun barrel in my mouth . . .

Then Tessie, my little Jack Russell, came bounding up to me out of nowhere, just as she had so many times before. It changed the blackest mood I've ever had in an instant. I thought, out here, with my dog, there's not a lot anyone can do to me. I thought of Tanya returning from the shops and finding me. Reality kicked in. I couldn't do it.

At first I couldn't tell Tans what I had gone through. It took me a few weeks before I told her exactly what had happened. She was so upset that it made the whole episode seem worse. She made it clear that I had to talk to her more when I had my back to the wall in future; I wasn't alone, and that was what marriage was about.

I did get sacked by the *News of the World*. I was told the day before I was due to play for Wimbledon in a Cup tie in Liverpool.

At the time, when the editor broke the news, it was like a boot in the stomach, but I was sure I'd be able to play – until I went to bed and couldn't sleep. So I got up, got in a car and drove straight back to Tanya.

The newspaper ran my version of events – with a picture of me with my head in my hands. They also ran a story across the back saying they'd sacked me.

This time, there was no FA disciplinary hearing as it had nothing directly to do with football.

I have never been back to those woods where Tessie distracted me from doing the unthinkable. I don't like going over old ground. And I decided to scramble out of the brambles and face the world.

The incident in Ireland was just the first episode of the dog misbehaving – more trouble was to come.

The eleventh red card of my career was waved in my face on a slippery pitch at Stamford Bridge after I went in on Dan Petrescu and then Ruud Gullit.

A couple of press boys waiting for me at home afterwards asked me about it and – *wham!* – I let go. A big show appeared the next day about me complaining that foreign players were 'squealing like pot-bellied pigs'. I still feel that a lot of foreign players do make too much of the slightest touch, but it created another huge outcry.

The following season, 1996–7, was to see Wimbledon in reach of Wembley again – making the semis of both the League (sponsored by Coca-Cola then and called the Coca-Cola Cup) and FA Cups. But it all started in familiar fashion for me with another red card as we chalked up our first Premiership victory of the season, by the only goal at home to Tottenham. I was booked first because of my fury after I caught Darren Anderton spitting. I thought he was gobbing at me and I went for him. I was fuming and went after him for the rest of the match – until I was red-carded.

We were put out of the FA Cup in a semifinal against Chelsea at Highbury and I just can't explain it. It was as if we'd inherited the feeling of the Liverpool team when we so gloriously battered them – listless, bored, restless. And I couldn't even get worked up leaving the ground. I can't explain that. It just wasn't the same for me – all the familiar faces I had loved had gone and the camaraderie had changed. Guys like Warren Barton were there and the quality in the squad wasn't what I had been used to at Leeds and Chelsea. Wimbledon did plenty more losing during my final season with them, 1997–8. The results were poor, we scraped through the season but became whipping boys in a lot of games.

My departure still leaves me with a lump in my throat. When you have so much history with a club, winning the FA Cup and captaining the side, it is always going to pull on the heartstrings when you leave. It really did signal the end of an era for me, and I knew I had to move on to something new.

But I had a great opportunity to learn the ropes as a manager by going to Queens Park Rangers as a player/coach.

Manager Ray Harford asked me to pick his brains, and I did. He told me there was every chance to move me into coaching and management. The dread of being finished in football, which was suddenly before me, was too much, so I seized the chance with both hands.

By this stage, I owned a thing or two. I didn't have a wardrobe before I became a footballer. Now I had suits made. I had my shoes hand-made. I used to have one gun; now I had fourteen for all the different types of shooting. I had invested in a promotional company, an IT firm and property. I'd bought the vehicles of my dreams, a top-of-the-line Range Rover, a Toyota truck; Tans had a brand-new BMW; and my job at QPR came with a new Merc. I got my sister two or three cars over the years; and Dad has had a Jeep.

We moved to Box Moor in July. I was technically two years away from retirement and spending big on a new house. The unfortunate story behind the move was trouble with the neighbours. I was accused of assaulting one of them in a row about removing a farm gate from my land.

One night in the cells was bad enough after the bust-up, but what followed was a living nightmare. I always felt confident I'd be cleared of the charges – actual bodily harm and criminal damage – and that was the feeling when I arrived at St Albans Magistrates' Court at the start of June with Tanya, sister Ann, Mum and Dad, my mother- and father-in-law.

I was found guilty.

I had to return to court a month later and in the meantime became convinced they were going to put me away. I knew I could cope with prison but I worried about Tanya and the family. I was also worried I'd be sacked from QPR, where I'd been made assistant manager.

I was conscious of how much money I had set aside, most of it tied up in property. I had always had good commercial deals that added to my salary, but I found a lot of them were cancelled after the fight with my neighbour. I had a two-and-a-half-year deal at QPR still to run on £7,500 a week, and was aware that that had to be paid off if I left the club. That being said, I was accustomed to a good standard of living with the family, and the big football wages wouldn't be coming in for ever, so I was aware I needed a Plan B.

I drank more in those weeks than I ever have. I wanted the company in the pubs and I wanted to forget.

We moved house the day before I went to court to learn my fate. When I heard the words, 'We are not considering a custodial sentence,' I floated away with elation.

Instead it was a hundred hours' community service and a fine and costs of £1,150. I ended up painting and decorating an old people's home.

It seemed then my future was with QPR. I couldn't foresee the events that were about to change everything.

My last ever professional football match – although I didn't know it at the time – was for QPR reserves away to Swindon. That game was like a summary of my entire career – from the sublime to the ridiculous. I smashed in a twenty-five-yard worldy, as we would have called it, and then got myself sent off in the same half. Here's the thing: it wasn't a sending-off. The referee accused me of throwing an elbow into a player behind me. That's bollocks – I was holding him off and defending myself with my arms up; it was all within the laws of the game in my opinion. At the time it was hard for me to take, and I didn't know it was going to be the end of my career.

We played at Oxford on a Saturday towards the end of September. I was told to sit it out because of events in the reserves' match at Swindon. I wanted to play in the Oxford game. Instead I watched Oxford beat QPR easily.

That was to be the last time I saw the lads. I blew my top at them in the dressing room afterwards, yelling that it showed a total lack of professionalism and will to win. I felt disillusioned within four months of joining QPR.

The manager, Ray Harford, quit afterwards. But they stuck Iain Dowie in charge – even though I'd been Ray's No. 2. I had joined on the understanding I'd be boss if he left or moved on. I told the execs I was thirty-four and wanted a crack at management – my way. Even now I'm gutted that they didn't give me my chance.

I remember one of the players coming round to my house with a bin liner, the good old bin liner again, with all my boots, training kit and flip-flops. QPR had asked me to train with the kids and I knew that was it. Gerry Francis came in to manage the club, called me up and told me I wasn't in his plans as a player and that he wanted his own coaching staff. That was it – game over. I'd come from being captain of Wimbledon to QPR, and suddenly it was all over. I was fully committed to QPR and it hurt me that the players were in cliques. I was used to a certain level of commitment and dedication as a professional player: I trained hard and kept in good shape. Razor Ruddock and I had been drafted in to save the club from relegation the season before as players – and we delivered that. I think we could have built on that and taken the club on, but, by the stage *Lock, Stock and Two Smoking Barrels* was coming (see Chapter 10), I knew they wanted me out. They booted me right in the teeth. Their only excuse seemed to be my involvement in a film that was to change my life – but at that point I was broken. I was told to find another club, but interest came from the lower divisions. They all wanted me to come in and liven them up. But I'd been at the top level too long.

After a lot of wrangling, I finally agreed with QPR to be paid another four months' wages and I walked away. I later found out that I had been stabbed in the back. Someone had gone round the players and whispered in their ears that I was going to get rid of them if I became the gaffer. I'll never forget that he did that and it hurt when QPR fans had a pop when I left and said I 'raped' the club for taking £750,000 as a payoff. The fact is, I could have taken more, considering I had two and half years left on my contract. Chris Wright, the chief exec, has written his own book and he showed me the chapter about that time. He actually apologises to me in it. We went for lunch at the Ivy in LA and managed to talk it all through, so I'm glad we made peace.

As I look back, it seems funny how they brought up the part in *Lock, Stock* as an excuse – but it actually did change my life. It was just something that appealed, but I never thought it would take me where it did.

I don't have a chip on my shoulder. I have a dislike of some of the people who ran QPR. The criticism had been hard to take along the way. And what a way to bow out of professional football: Swindon reserves away with a red card. Then a bin bag with your boots and not even a handshake from the club – just a cheque that meant nothing. Thank God Jerry Bruckheimer had made that call: who knows where I would have ended up without it?

But there is one person who will be looking down on all this with a smile on his face: Granddad Arthur Jones.

I still talk to him. And when things started kicking off in my new career, I had a word.

10

Lock, Stock and Two Smoking Barrels

Towards the end of my playing career with Wimbledon, and then when I became assistant manager at QPR in 1998, my off-field interests really started to grow.

I had dabbled a bit with appearances on TV over the years. There was the *Soccer's Hard Men* DVD in 1992, which ended up costing me a few quid and a ban from the game. My agent's business partner, Jeff Weston, had told me about a video that was being put together about soccer's hard men – a few talking heads from the game discussing the muck and bullets of football. I was at Sheffield United at the time and was offered £2,000, less my agent's fee, which was 20 per cent. So I agreed.

That video went on to sell well over a hundred thousand

copies, with my face plastered across the front. The FA accused me of bringing the game into disrepute and they decided to make an example of me. I had a hearing in front of the FA, a selection of about eight gentlemen in their eighties, who decided to clobber me with a £20,000 fine – the biggest the game had seen at that time. They also gave me a six-month ban, suspended for three years. They didn't even flinch when I offered my defence about all the work I did with grassroots players and kids' charities.

Then one of the early Sky channels, Men & Motors, had given me a shot at my own interview show. Some bright spark let me come up with the celebrities to interview and off we went. At one point it looked as if we had Mike Tyson in the bag, but for whatever reason it never came off. Instead, I kicked off my onscreen interviewing career by talking to Charlton Heston.

I was told I would have only four minutes at a junket in the Dorchester hotel in London – and we ended up chatting for a good fifteen minutes. Afterwards, his publicist told me he loved the interview. Charlton Heston liked Vinnie Jones! I couldn't believe it. Others followed: Damon Hill, Mickey Duff and Peter Stringfellow inside his club in Leicester Square.

I got a few football-related chats too: former Arsenal player and manager Terry Neill and top-flight referee David Elleray.

The whole idea of the show was to create the feel of blokes chatting down at the pub. Funnily enough, I didn't find it too taxing! Was I successful? I was only voted New Presenter of the Year at the Sky awards! But little did I realise that winning that poxy award was to give me the opportunity to completely change my life.

It all began with a phone call to my agent, from a couple of blokes called Guy Ritchie and Matthew Vaughn. (Ring any bells?) They had seen a few bits of my TV work – particularly a tiny speaking part in a show called *Ellington*, in which I played a mouthy footballer – what a stretch! – and wanted to sound me out about having a cameo in their low-budget gangster Brit flick they were working on. It was called *Lock, Stock and Two Smoking Barrels*.

Appearing in films had never been on my radar before but I've always loved the cinema. Tans and I had recently seen *Train-spotting* together. That was an eye-opener. (Years later I had a night out with one of its stars, Ewan McGregor, when he was still on the drink – it was a messy one – at some Donatella Versace bash.) I was definitely intrigued by Guy and Matthew's enquiry, and the more I thought about it the more I realised I really fancied it.

My manager arranged for me to meet them at Stoke Park House, in Stoke Poges, Bucks. This was the golf course where James Bond – Sean Connery at the time – fought Oddjob in *Goldfinger*. Not a bad place for my first movie meeting.

It was the first time I had ever set eyes on the pair of them. Guy was the writer and director, Matthew the producer, and I could tell they were a bit nervous. The truth is, I was nervous too. After a quick chat, they took me to a shooting range nearby so we could talk guns. It was a key part of the story and they knew I had a bit of experience from a bit of research they had done.

The notes about my character, Big Chris, had described him as 'respected but you wouldn't want to cross this man. Similar to Vinnie Jones the footballer.'

The more we chatted, the more I realised I was desperate to land this role. Guy and Matthew both seemed keen but they warned me there was someone else I'd have to impress. Her name was Celestia Fox – some top casting director who had apparently discovered Arnold Schwarzenegger. Bloody hell! No pressure, then!

After training one day, I went up to the ICM talent agency's office on Tottenham Court Road to meet them all. I'm not ashamed to say I was bricking it.

We were in these beautiful offices and Celestia was sitting there at this big table, full of herself, a proper Hollywood power dresser. I went in, didn't know how to deal with the situation, so I began by doing the part of the script for Big Chris I'd memorised. 'Yes, Harry. No, Harry, you can't' and 'Come and see me – you better be waving the white flag.'

Celestia took a few breaths then finally said something: 'It's OK . . .'

OK? OK? OK wasn't going to get me into the movies.

Celestia then took Guy and Matthew outside. I thought I might have blown it. My one shot, gone.

But not long after that she came back and said, 'Now, do it as yourself. Not as Big Chris. Do it as Vinnie Jones, as if you were talking to mates in the pub.'

So I did – and she was over the moon with the result. I'd done it – the part was mine.

Lock, Stock was a gangster movie with a real sense of humour. It was a great plot and story, with some excellent characters – but best of all it made you laugh. The timing and editing were world-class – with a classic cliffhanger of an ending.

Most of my scenes were shot in and around Brick Lane. There was nothing done in fancy studios, or any clever green-screen business: this was all straightforward, spit-and-sawdust stuff, with someone watching the clock – if someone could afford one – because the budget was so tight. Some of the scenes were done at 4 a.m., so I would be driven to the set, then I'd put my hoody up and whiz home on the train.

I filmed the majority of the movie when I was playing for Wimbledon. All the lads used to come down to Plough Lane because I ran the players' bar. It was part of my job as captain. They loved it and it played a big part in our bonding as a gang.

In fact, I remember going to an away game with Wimbledon around this time. One of the lads had brought a video along with him and said we should all watch it before the game. We were sitting in the bus completely gripped by it. It was so good that when we got to the hotel we sat in the coach for another forty minutes so we could watch it without interruption. It was *The Shawshank Redemption* and it blew my mind. I went on to work with Morgan Freeman, who played one of the inmates in the movie, and I remember telling him the story.

With *Lock, Stock*, because the process of making it took so long to get going, I was at QPR by the time it was released – and it couldn't have come at a better time. I've often wondered what I would have done if it had all run on time. Would I have turned down Hollywood for the last couple of years as a player? I still don't know the answer, even now.

We were well down the road with filming when everything stopped and seemed to have gone down the pan. They had some problems financing the film, which meant a lot of the actors pulled out who had originally said yes.

I don't think I realised at the time just how tight things were for Guy and Matthew. Matthew explained to me years later that they were shitting themselves at our initial Stoke Poges meeting in case we wanted lunch, because they didn't know whether the credit card would go through!

The film fell down another couple of times but they finally came back to me and said they had the money. I was like, 'Look boys, I'm here.' So they locked me in. I stayed loyal to them when everyone else was jumping ship. I'm sure Nick Moran got the role as Eddy only a few days before things started rolling again.

Guy and Matthew also remained loyal to me, because during that downtime I found myself in the cells over the incident with my then neighbour in Hemel Hempstead. As I mentioned earlier, I lost a lot of work over that conviction, but Guy and Matthew stuck by me.

When things eventually got going, it took nine weeks of filming. I was standing around all day and acting for about five minutes, but I really enjoyed it. They were great people to work with and it gave me the taste for more.

The first day on set I was measured for the clothes I was going to wear. I didn't know anyone from Adam. It wasn't very glamorous for a film set. Jason Flemyng – who played Tom – was the first actor I met. The only other person I had shaken hands with by that point was Lenny McLean, the notorious London bareknuckle fighter, when we went for our medical. He played Barry the Baptist, who was Hatchet Harry's minder.

My first ever acting scene in a movie was the famous sunbed scene. I had to knock seven bells out of a lad by smashing the top half of the sunbed on him. The actor was Jimmy Tarbuck's son!

Guy had auditioned lots of kids to play my son, Little Chris. The first line he had was, 'Fucking hell – you must have a monkey here,' but all the kids were coming in with their parents and didn't want to swear. The lad who eventually got the part, Peter McNicholl, came in with his brother, who was a DJ. He was a cocky little shit and Guy knew straight away he was our boy. He said it as if he'd been saying it all his life. We wanted my son Aaron to do it, but he was just a bit too young.

That first scene was a bloody nightmare because the sunbed just kept falling apart. I don't know whether Matthew or Guy tried to rig it up before – a DIY thing – but every time you moved it, the whole thing was falling off and knocking the fella on the head.

I had a runner on the film called Adi, who looked after me. He would pick me up in the morning and help me out if I needed anything. There was another scene where I was just sitting in the car waiting. I used to smoke cigars then, Hamlet and Classics, so for some reason I started to smoke in the scene. The thing was, all the cigars were my own – they didn't buy them in as props. So I was running out of cigars, told Adi to run to the shop for me and get me a couple of packets. I didn't know at the time I could have just said to them we needed them as props. So, anyway, we go to film the scene, me sitting in this Cobra motor, late at night, and we only really had the money for a couple of takes, it was so tight. What I hadn't told anyone was that, when I had jumped into the car, my trousers had split from my crotch to the back of my arse, right the way round. So I was sitting there, trying to be an actor.

After my line, they cut and I couldn't get out of the car. Everyone was in stitches. The cameras started rolling again and Adi comes running over. 'Vin, Vin, I've got your cigars!' Guy's screaming at him to get off the set. It was fucking hilarious. It was like *Fawlty Towers*, it really was.

I never used to wear socks then, even in winter. I hated them, still do. The funny thing that none of them could get over was that it was freezing cold and I'm standing outside having a cup of tea with Lenny McLean and I've got no socks on. I don't wear socks in any scene in *Lock, Stock* – there's a bit of trivia for really big fans of the film.

In the original movie, my role was a lot smaller. They decided to cut out the role of Eddy's girlfriend and Guy said to me, 'I'm making your character a lot bigger. I've loved what you've done.'

I was blown away. My first film and I'd done a good job!

Jason Flemyng actually put his own money in to make the film. He was there all the time, but at the time I couldn't understand why if he wasn't acting in that scene. He took me in to the back of the truck one day to show me a little bit I'd done. He said, 'Oh, Vin, it's brilliant. I'm telling you, fucking great job.' Years later I found out Flem had invested in the film. He really helped with my acting. He kept reminding me what Celestia Fox had said to me: 'Just be yourself.'

There was a great bit of banter with P. H. Moriarty, who played Hatchet Harry. He was in a *Jaws* film. I'm like, 'Fucking hell. This is a real fucking actor.' But PH is very much a real geezer.

We were doing the scene where Hatchet Harry is in his office and his desk is covered in sex toys. Before we started filming the scene, I grabbed the big black dildo on the desk. While he was having his makeup done, I lodged it between my legs and just stood there.

Now I've got to do a bit of dialogue with him and I haven't told anyone about my extra 'prop'.

He's being really serious and Guy shouts, 'Ready PH?' He replies, 'Yeah, ready, Guy.'

'Action!'

I'm just standing there. He's going, 'I can't have that, can I, Chris?' And I reply, 'No, Harry, you can't.' Just then, he looks down and sees this massive dildo dangling between my legs – and goes fucking berserk! It's stopped his dialogue, so he's spitting mad. He now knows this is one of my first days, so he's ranting at Guy. Now everybody's burst out laughing. We're all in this tiny little room and it's boiling hot, everyone is sweating and creasing up. He goes into one. 'I'm not having this! I'm used to working with fucking professionals!' He moves everything out the way, walks out, slamming the door off its hinges.

I just look round at everyone. Everybody had tears streaming. Guy told me to apologise. I went down to the tea trolley where PH was and said sorry. He was lovely, gave me a cuddle and said, 'It's all right my boy. But, you know, when I get into it and all that . . .'

When filming was finally wrapped up, they had a small screening for us all to have a look. I took my secretary, Lorraine, who helped out running the house for us and keeping on top of my diary, and Tans. We went up to see it and as we sat in Euston Station afterwards, Tans said, 'Vin, that is the funniest thing I've ever seen. This is going to be massive.' I couldn't believe it.

Lorraine then piped up: 'Vin, it's so funny.'

So the girls obviously saw something.

Little did I know that this low-budget gangster movie was about to blow up in a big way – and lead to massive movie roles.

11

Lock, Stock and Two Smoking Barrels II

I had absolutely no idea of the impact *Lock, Stock* would make. It changed the nature and direction of my life to the point where a younger generation didn't know I was famous for winning the FA Cup. It was just something I was invited to do, something that appealed, but I never anticipated what would happen once it was in the cinemas.

I felt as if I had done a decent job for a first-time effort but it wasn't until later that I began to think I might have a future in Hollywood.

Dustin Hoffman was on the red carpet at the London premiere. I had my picture taken with him and he mentioned something about 'the new Bruce Willis'. Maybe he was just being kind but, as we chatted and I turned around, I saw my dad with tears of pride streaming down his face. The floodgates had opened again. Tanya showed her emotions by giggling all the way through it. After I'd received more than my fair share of criticism as a footballer, it was nice to be picking up the papers and reading, 'Vinnie Jones's contribution to the movie was impressive.'

The whole production had been a really low-budget affair but the boys had some friends in high places. Steve Tisch, who had produced *Forrest Gump* and some other huge Hollywood hits, arranged for the film to be shown in LA with a big premiere because he had seen the movie and loved it.

Peter Morton, who had a lot of money in the Hard Rock Cafe chain, was another huge supporter. He lumped in with Stephen Marks, from FCUK, and they covered the costs to make sure we had a big event to mark the release in Tinseltown.

Peter Morton looked after us in style out there. He arranged for a private jet to take me, Guy, Matthew and Jay from Burbank Airport to Vegas. We were picked up in a limo, taken onto the runway, escorted onto the plane, then it was the same treatment at the other end. We were dropped off at the Hard Rock Cafe, where Santana were playing, where we had the best seats in the house. I remember Peter roaring onto the runway in a blue Ferrari to come and join us. Carlos Santana came on stage, played a song and said, 'I'd like to extend a huge Vegas welcome to our friends from the UK who are starring in a huge new movie, *Lock, Stock and Two Smoking Barrels.*' We all stood up and gave the place a wave. It was incredible. He flew us back that night to LA, where he had put all our names down on the Sky Bar at the Mondrian – it was the first time I had ever been there. We felt as if we had landed in the big leagues.

While I was out in Los Angeles I was introduced to lots of people – casting agents at Paramount and Warner – and I began to think this could be the way I was going to make a living after football, because people were dishing out compliments and a couple of scripts arrived. We were flown around all over the place, first-class, limousines here, there and everywhere, private jets to Las Vegas and back for lunch. And in the end I won a few awards: the Empire Variety Club of Great Britain, the Odeon Cinemas Award. *Lock, Stock* was winning them as well. I was going to all the functions and becoming friends with people like Michael Caine and Bob Hoskins. I found myself accepted by all the big hitters.

I met Bob right at the beginning. I had a little chat and he said, 'I'm really impressed, Vin. You can do this. You need to start thinking whether you want to do it properly, because you can earn a good living at this.' I always remember that he said, 'Your screen presence is immense.' Imagine hearing that from Bob the legend Hoskins.

Big movie stars were taking an interest in me and wanted to be friends. When I was young, I used to run if there was a group I didn't feel part of. With the movie business, I felt as if I belonged.

For years in football, I was angry with the game, angry with the pundits and, a lot of the time, angry with the journalists writing about me. All that changed when I got my break in movies. I learned a valuable lesson from the off on *Lock, Stock*. You have to make the most of it while it lasts.

On the night of the LA premiere, the first major A-lister I saw was (the late) Patrick Swayze. He was walking the red carpet.

For me to recognise someone, they've got to be big – my daughter Kaley will tell you that. I am useless at recognising people – she always has to tell me who they are after they have come over and said hello. Anyway, I couldn't believe it was the geezer out of *Ghost*. The PR woman was saying, 'Patrick, can you move along now please.' That was a Hollywood lesson – one minute you are cock of the walk, the next minute they are moving you on for a one-time hod carrier from Bedmond to have his say with the assembled media.

We *Lock, Stock* boys were all treating the premiere as if it were the first and last time we would ever be there. It was our moment in LA and it was something special. They had red buses and the red carpet was a shambles because we were just causing major bollocks.

Jason Statham, Guy Ritchie, Matthew Vaughn and I had come over together. It was my first time in LA and we flew in first-class to LAX. My first ever sight of it sticks with me – this grid system. We came in over Hollywood Park Race Track and I was thinking, Fucking hell. This'll do me!

We were put up in the Four Seasons, all expenses paid, for a week. Sting was there with us – he played Eddy's dad JD in the film – and he is a fantastic geezer, absolutely brilliant. Such a cool man. After *Lock, Stock*, his missus Trudie Styler gave me this beautiful tie, with flowers on it. I've still got it framed. It said, 'To Vinnie. Congratulations on your new career. All our love, The Sumner Babes x'.

A few months after the premiere, Tans, I and a few other people had gone to Ago, Robert De Niro's restaurant, for a spot of dinner. We were sitting in there and I didn't know Sting was in too. The waiter came over with a bottle of Dom Perignon wrapped in a serviette. I said, 'Who's this from?' He said, 'There's a message on there, Mr Jones.' So I've opened it up and it was signed on the serviette in capital letters: 'TO VINNIE. CONGRATULATIONS ON YOUR NEW CAREER. LOVE, THE SUMNER BABES X'.

They were sitting at the back of the restaurant and they'd sent it over. So I went over and had a good craic with them. Trudie and Sting made a big fuss of us as they were leaving.

But that first LA trip was an extension of the football camaraderie I had enjoyed throughout my career. It was hilarious at the Four Seasons. On the first night there, we were out on the patio at 2 a.m., no press had been done and we hadn't even had the premiere. We were having a good drink, dancing away and doing all the Irish songs, and then someone who I thought was Sandra Bullock came out and started shouting at us at the top of her voice. She was going for it: 'Can you lot give it up, for God's sake – I am trying to get some sleep in here.' Turns out it wasn't Sandra Bullock – it was Liz Hurley.

After the press conference on the day we were due to leave, I went to the gift shop and re-enacted a trick the Wimbledon lads used to do in hotels at away games. I decided to treat myself and put it on someone else's bill. Jason Statham was on the receiving end. The prices were fucking ridiculous. I've gone in the shop and nearly cleared it out! I walked away with all this stuff, from jewellery boxes and trinkets to chocolate and T-shirts. I got presents for everyone back home and signed it to Statham's room! He came down later while we were all round the pool and he was going fucking ballistic. I asked, 'What's up Jay?' He said,

'Some fucker's put about three grand's worth of stuff on my room out the fucking gift shop, that's what.' Then he added, 'Jones, was that you?'

I said, 'Were there any cigars on it?'

'No,' he chirped back.

'Well, how was it me, then?'

I've still got the jewellery box I bought in my house some-where.

There was a real similarity between the way the *Lock, Stock* boys were and the Crazy Gang scenario we had at Wimbledon. I'm still really close to Jay, the other Jason – Flemyng – Guy and Matthew. Dexter Fletcher? Well, our paths have not really crossed since, but I love Dex. He's a good lad. I think most people's careers changed with that movie. Even as far as the wardrobe department and makeup. I think 99 per cent of the people have earned a good living since.

After *Lock, Stock*, I no longer wanted to be Vinnie the foot-baller, I wanted to be Vinnie the film star. The *Lock, Stock* boys became like family after that. I was looking after them because none of them had much money of their own. I used to have them all down to the football and sort the hospitality out. We all got close early on after Guy asked me up to the offices to have a card school. Three-card brag was my game, so they wanted me to come up and show them how it was done.

Guy had really looked after me right from the moment he asked me to do the role in *Lock, Stock* and he helped set me up with the ICM talent agency.

Guy's dad was the fella who wrote all the Hamlet commercials and he had pulled a favour with Duncan Heath, one of the biggest and best agents in the UK. He looks after Dame Maggie Smith, Gary Oldman, Alan Rickman and Sir Michael Caine – and then he went on to represent me too.

It was a stroke of genius from Guy to introduce us. Duncan was well into greyhound racing, as was I, so he knew it was a good connection to make.

Things all happened so fast for me – it was like a whirlwind. We were in a tornado and, once the film came out, things just blew up. It was the hottest ticket in town. I was still at QPR, of course, and the manager, Ray Harford, was literally begging me for a ticket! I took him and Iain Dowie to the UK premiere.

We knew the industry would turn their nose up at us, which they did, but the punters thought it was very funny and that's what really counts.

The LA premiere was one of those moments I knew I had to savour at the time, a bit like the unbelievable night we won the FA Cup final.

And that's how I felt about the success of *Lock, Stock*. I was made up that this top bunch of lads, my film family, had come up with a big hit – and I wanted more.

Thankfully, the film's success meant it wasn't long before all of us were back together making another British gangster film – only this time with a little bit of Hollywood A-list sparkle thrown in.

12

Snatch

A career in films is a lot like a career in football. When you start off and make your debut, you feel the butterflies, and your success depends on how well you channel the fear and nervous energy. I always used to get the butterflies before a game, but I learned how to handle my nerves. Making movies was the same for me. I found my confidence and started to enjoy it. The only challenge I really faced was learning dialogue, so I approached that as I approached training for football: put the hours in and all the hard work and you will know your stuff. That took care of it all for me.

It would be fair to say I caught the acting bug after *Lock, Stock*. That was it for me – I wanted to leave football behind and make it as a movie star. All through my football career, I felt I didn't get a fair crack of the whip from a lot of the football writers – even guys I thought were good friends. It always jarred with me because I felt as if I was underrated – you look at my time at Leeds and I guarantee manager Howard Wilkinson and captain Gordon Strachan would vouch for my ability as a player.

Suddenly, post-*Lock, Stock*, I was getting good reviews and really felt wanted, brushing shoulders with the famous, but what was more important to me was that I was being recognised for having some ability and presence on screen. Even towards the end of filming *Lock, Stock*, there was another gangster movie lined up involving the same crowd from Ska Films.

But *Lock, Stock*'s success meant the new movie – *Snatch* – was definitely a goer. Quietly, I didn't want just another part in the film: I wanted to be the star of it. I knew that I had more to offer and, without the distraction of football, or of grief at QPR, I could turn it into a springboard for my new career. I knew and sensed I was in with a shout of a decent part after the success of our first film together – we had a winning formula and we were all brimming with confidence. Guy had been working on the script at the time we were shooting *Lock, Stock* and I could tell from our conversations he had me in mind. The lads had Ska Films' offices in the West End and we would all congregate around there. We all knew about *Snatch* pretty quickly and there was a bit of jostling for position for the roles.

In the very early stages of *Snatch* being discussed, I actually met Kelly Brook for the first time. I'd gone down to the offices and in walked Guy, Matthew Vaughn, Jason Statham and this gorgeous young girl – Kelly. I think she was seventeen at the time. Absolutely gorgeous.

So Stath comes over to me and goes, 'Look at this. They're all trying their bollocks off.'

A few days later I get a phone call from Stath: 'Jonesy, Jonesy. Remember that bird Kelly? I'm going to take her out.'

I was like, 'Go on, son!'

But I've only got my old van,' he said, 'I can't fucking pick her up in that. What do I do?'

So I said, 'Jump on the train, come down to Hemel to me.'

I had a few motors back then. As part of my QPR deal I got a Mercedes. So I said to him, 'I've got this Merc here, borrow it.'

So that's what he did. Took the car, had it for a few days and he fucking cracked it!

Kelly and Stath were with each other for seven years, after that. I had all that heartache with him over her when they split. I was with him when all that came out. We were up at the Four Seasons again in LA and I thought he was going to throw himself off the balcony. That's when the close 'family' comes in.

Anyway, while we were all putting our pitches in to Guy for the roles in *Snatch*, there was one new fella who jumped the queue to bag one of the lead spots. I would have been livid about it – but that fella was Brad Pitt.

When we all heard that Brad was coming on board, I was like, 'Wahey! Here we go, Jonah, old son, this is it.' The cast on *Lock, Stock* was impressive, but made up of a lot of new faces. Brad Pitt was getting involved with *Snatch* at a time when his stock couldn't have been higher. I mean, even *I* knew who he was!

With *Snatch*, the whole gang became really good friends. We used all the same crew and makeup people, so, when we started filming, it was basically like the beginning of term but with a few new kids in the class. It just so happened one of the new kids was one of the most famous actors in the world – and one of the best in the business at that. It also turned out that he was a truly top geezer. In my football career, I came up against some big names in the game, huge personalities who carried a reputation around with them. As far as I was concerned, I was going into the new film with exactly the same attitude. I felt as if I had earned this role through my work on *Lock, Stock* and it was a chance to impress. All eyes would be on Brad Pitt, especially in Hollywood, so I knew that, if I put in a good shift, it was going to be a door opening.

When filming finally got under way – there was no mucking about with funding as we had on *Lock, Stock* – things got off to a pretty good start, and we had some great card games in Brad's trailer. It was like the focal point of the set and was a marker for what was to come.

I got friendly with Brad pretty quickly. He would call me up and I remember the first time my daughter Kaley clocked who she was talking to. Most of the calls would go through the house because mobile phones were only just getting big. He rang the house once when Kaley was about thirteen. She was being a typical grumpy teenager and gave him a hard time. She had no idea who it was and eventually asked for his name. I heard her fall off the bed! Then she came running through shouting, 'It's Brad Pitt on the phone! Oh my God!' It's funny to think that, even up until a couple of years ago, Brad would still ring me up from time to time. I used to go round to his house to play cards, which seems to have been a great icebreaker, from football all the way through the movies.

For anyone who hasn't seen *Snatch*, Brad played a double-hard traveller and bare-knuckle fighter called Mickey O'Neil. It was a completely different role from what he was used to playing. It couldn't have been further from the clean-cut poster-boy parts he was always being linked with. Brad wanted to crack the traveller dialogue and sound as authentic as he could, so I arranged for him to spend time with some real Gypsies – the Frankham family – near to where I grew up. I just phoned Jonny Frankham up and he said, 'Yeah, that'll be all right.'

For some reason, I couldn't be there with Brad on the day we sorted it, so the boys took him down to the site near Watford. For anyone who hasn't seen the film – or an episode of *My Big Fat Gypsy Wedding* on television – a Gypsy site can be an intimidating and brutal place to find yourself. This was a Hollywood A-lister, staying at the Dorchester at the time, so it must have been a shock to his system.

I had asked Matthew Vaughn to look after Jonny and keep an eye on Brad. So, anyway, they went up there and I was phoning to make sure everything was all right – there was always the prospect of funny business. No answer. They had arranged to be on site for a couple of hours. I called again, same thing – no answer. I waited another few hours and called back – still nothing. After eight hours I got hold of Matthew. It turns out Brad slipped right into it – and absolutely loved every minute down there! Matthew said Brad didn't want to leave and he was running around with all the kids, kicking footballs about and spinning along on a BMX. He even sat down to have something to eat with them all. I thought that said a lot about the fella. It definitely ingratiated him with all of us – there were no airs or graces, or the ego you might expect. He really got into it and cracked on.

The Gypsy family sold all their pictures to the tabloids and at the time I felt a bit awkward because I had made the introduction. Luckily, Brad was completely cool with it: it was great publicity for the film, after all.

One night during filming, he called me up and said, 'Hey, Vin, what are you doing?' I was finishing up a game of golf or something and was planning a night at the dogs. I said, 'I'm going to Walthamstow dogs, Brad.'

He went, 'I'm bored out of my mind in the hotel. Can I meet you there?'

Well it's not a difficult one is it?

'Of course,' I told him.

He said, 'Great.'

I said, 'We have a table there, we have a steak and all the family are coming.'

He passed the phone over to his driver and I told him the score. Brad had only one bodyguard on the film, which, looking back on it, was brave. He was at the top of his game and Walthamstow could get quite lively.

I loved it at the dogs – Harry Redknapp and Joe Kinnear were regulars at Walthamstow. A good few characters liked a night down there.

Anyway, on this night, we got Brad upstairs and sat him down at 'our' table – I used to have my table right in the corner, always the same one. So we got plotted up in there and the staff started coming over. People actually thought I had brought a Brad Pitt lookalike at first! They thought I was having a wind-up, because it wasn't well known that we were in a film together.

We had a great night and all of a sudden it all clicked between us. Brad did all the pictures, autographs – everything that he was asked for. He had a great time. I sometimes wonder whether he's been to the dogs since.

Filming the movie during the day was such a great time. By then, I was comfortable around a film set and knew exactly what it was all about, how to go about it and get the best out of myself. My son Aaron, or Spud, as I call him, came on set quite a lot during *Snatch*. I've got some great pictures of him directing a scene with Guy where my character, Bullet Tooth Tony, has a horrible car crash. That was his directorial debut – at the ripe old age of ten!

The *Snatch* premiere in London was brilliant, especially because the studio put us all up in suites at the Dorchester. I was quite close to Brad by this point. We all were. On the night of the premiere, the railings collapsed in Leicester Square because there was a mad rush by fans desperate to touch him. Security had to whisk him away because it was getting too dangerous. I hadn't seen such hysteria for a famous face since I first came across Gazza when he was making a name for himself at Newcastle.

I hired eight limos from my house for all my mates to come along. I had an old mate of mine, Gary Bunning, on the red carpet with me. He is this massive bald-headed geezer. At the end of the night, I went out to get my limo home and he had taken it on his own! I was stuck in town and had to get a black cab back.

Around the time of the premiere, the story was hitting the papers about Guy and Madonna becoming a serious item. We were all at the official after party together – but Madonna wanted to throw her own, which I was dead against at the time. I said, 'This is bollocks. How can you invite some and not others?' We were told, 'Well, that's how it is.'

In the end, most of us went along to Madonna's party. It was at some swanky club and, to be fair, we had another great night. She made a fuss of Seamus and Cal – two of my oldest friends in the world. Cal is attending Harefield now for his heart problems, the same hospital Tans spent so much time in. It's funny to think we had spent so much of our time boozing and fighting, then here we were with Madonna, living it up.

We told her and Guy the story of our friendship and they thought it was great, how we had all remained friends through thick and thin. It was a real clash of cultures and social status that night. You would have my lads at the bar drinking next to Quentin Tarantino. He came up to me and said what a great job I had done and all that. Imagine hearing that from Quentin Tarantino.

The lovely thing for me was that all the celebrities there and all the important studio executives were flying in to Brad for a handshake and a hug. He would stop them in their tracks and go, 'This is Vinnie. He played Bullet Tooth Tony.' He brought everybody into it. Brad was just fantastic, so cool.

At the premiere everyone was talking about Alan Ford, or Brick Top, as he was in the film. Tarantino loved him and I'm surprised they haven't worked together. I thought his career was going to fly. Alan wasn't originally meant to go to the LA premiere, but I had a word with Guy and Matthew and they arranged for him to fly over.

Alan's part was actually the one I really had my heart set on when I first read the script at home in Hemel. When Guy asked me what I thought of the script, I just told him, 'I'm Brick Top,' but he talked me out of it. I told Alan that later and I said I was glad I didn't get the part. He just knocked the socks out of it in the end.

I also said I was keen on playing Turkish. I loved the part. But again Guy said, 'I think Jason Statham's really well suited to that.'

I said, 'What shall I do then? The dishes?'

Bullet Tooth Tony came into the story only later on and, to be honest, I didn't want that part. I wanted to be one of the main characters.

Guy said, 'If you nail this part, it'll be memorable.'

Guy knows what he's talking about, so I went along with it. But, when the cast, crew and families all watched the film for the first time at a screening, I was seething. I watched and watched and watched – and Bullet Tooth Tony finally made an appearance almost halfway through.

I was livid. When you watch a film for the first time, you're not watching the plot: you're just waiting to see yourself. It can be quite a selfish mindset but that's just the way it goes.

The screening was at this exec producer called Steve Tisch's place in Los Angeles and I called Guy and Matthew up on the phone and went berserk.

I said, 'You bastards! What the fuck have you done?'

Guy went, 'Calm down!'

I said, 'Calm down? I'm hardly in the fucking movie! I feel embarrassed.'

Guy said, 'Listen. You don't realise how awesome you are in this, Vin. I promise you.'

Anyway, the next thing I know, I've won Best British Actor at the Empire Awards, beating Sir Michael Caine in the process. What does Guy know, eh?

Winning that award was amazing for me, in front of Ray Winstone and Michael, so I said a few words about how proud I felt to even be in their company. I'm conscious that I keep mentioning all these names, but I really was like a kid in the candy shop – and I still am.

As always, I had a brilliant night out afterwards. There was me, John Hurt, Michael Caine and Richard Harris. That's a serious team. We were at the bar at the Dorchester and we got fucking hammered in there.

But, even though I was hanging around with all these big names, I always made sure I looked after my old mates. I was out in LA for the US premiere of *Snatch* with Tans and my mate Tony Allen, a restaurateur, and something just didn't feel right. We were sitting on the patio at the Four Seasons and I turned to them both and said, 'What am I doing? My two closest mates that I've grown up with aren't here. I'm getting carried away with myself. They've got to be here with me. They've got to see this.'

I phoned up Lorraine, my secretary, and I told her to buy flight tickets for Cal and Seamus, and to go round to their house and give them the tickets and tell them they're coming the next day. I got them a room at the Four Seasons and, sure enough, the next day they came walking into the hotel on the day of the premiere. I was over the moon. I had my best mates with me and it didn't take long for things to get rowdy. The Four Seasons hadn't seen anything like it! A few Bedmond boys let loose in Beverly Hills! But that was exactly how I wanted it to be. The success that had started to come my way was incredible but, after everything I had battled through in my life to get there once in football, I was determined to make sure that, if I was going to be lucky twice, then all my original pals would be around me to get a piece of the action, too.

It's fair to say things were going pretty well for Vinnie Jones, the actor.

I'd won a couple of awards for the roles in *Lock, Stock* and *Snatch* and there had been a great honeymoon period with good reviews for everything I had done. I was riding the crest of a wave for a while. People were saying, 'He's great. What a great part.' It was brilliant for me and lifted my confidence. During my football career, I used to get the hump with football writers deciding the rating I was getting in the pub before I had even kicked a ball.

Now, in movies, everything seemed to be on the up. I felt invincible.

Then someone had to go and stick the boot in.

One evening I took a phone call from Paul Ridley, the old sports editor of the *Sun*. We were very good friends. We had been on holiday together, and he had this serious voice on, the one that I knew meant trouble. He said, 'There's a story coming tomorrow with Nick Moran.'

I was like, 'Oh, yeah?' And he broke the bad news that he had really slagged me off in the paper.

I honestly couldn't believe Nick had the fucking balls to do it at the time, when he knew fine well there was a very good chance we would run into each other again.

Rids wanted me to respond and hit back in the paper, but I couldn't stoop to the same level. This was the first time anyone had broken from the crowd and really upset the apple cart. We all earned minimal money, it was a big break for everybody and almost all of us respected the bond that came with it.

Rids faxed the piece over to me and I gave it a read. Nick was giving it the big one about coming from where I came from and he was saying, 'Vinnie's over in LA now, with a big cigar on, giving it all the big bananas when he should be in the pub with his mates because that's what I would do.' I couldn't believe what I was reading. Guy tried to diffuse it. He made efforts to get us together to talk it over, but my mind was made up. I know I look after my mates and haven't forgotten my roots. For Nick to suggest otherwise was just bang out of order.

He tried to wriggle out of it. I had fifteen years of difficult run-ins with the press under my belt by this point – he had about fifteen days! This all happened in 2000 and I haven't spoken to him since.

It was career suicide for him. I meet people now who ask me, 'Who was that guy, the lead in *Lock, Stock*?' I'll explain it was Nick Moran and they will ask, 'What happened to that guy?' Later on, I heard that Guy had smacked Nick at some do or other.

But during *Snatch*, and despite the Nick Moran business, things were rattling along nicely for me – and then the movie dream really starting coming alive.

Hollywood came calling.

13

Hollywood

The turn of the century and the bringing-in of the New Year in 2000 was a really exciting time for everyone who had been involved with the first two movies. We were all being linked with big projects in the newspapers and, for a lot of the lads, it was their first taste of real fame.

I was having big meetings all the time by this point and felt as if there was a solid future for me in Hollywood. I really felt as if I had arrived in the big time.

I was with the ICM talent agency's LA branch under a guy called Nick Stein. My UK agent, Duncan Heath, was the chairman of ICM and he felt like part of the family – he was with me since the beginning. Duncan told me I had to go to LA to have any hope of making a proper career out of acting, so I went over and signed with Nick. Suddenly, I had an LA agent and a London agent.

Even now, Duncan is like a grandfather figure to us. I was in LA for six months, went back to the UK, then went back again for six months. Duncan eventually said, 'Look, Vin. You've grown and your acting isn't going to be in the UK any more: it's going to be in Hollywood. So it's best all your stuff goes through Nick Stein and his office.'

I took Duncan's advice and things really started happening.

It was actually while I was still in the UK that I got a call on the phone saying Jerry Bruckheimer and director Dominic Sena wanted to see me.

The film business was still relatively new to me, so I didn't know what to expect when he said he would be making arrangements for me to fly to LA as soon as possible.

The next thing I knew, first-class British Airways flights had been sorted from London Heathrow to LAX. I packed a bag, took the flight, arrived in LA and was taken by limo to a meeting at Jerry's offices in Santa Monica.

He and his right-hand man, Chad Omen, were sitting behind the biggest desk I'd ever seen. We chatted for about half an hour about whether I'd liked working on *Lock, Stock*, how many takes I needed – just a chat.

I had been there only a couple of minutes before he started talking about a film he was making called *Gone in 60 Seconds* – a $100 million movie starring Nicolas Cage. I nearly fell off my chair. Me? In a $100 million movie? With Nicolas Cage? Madness!

They wanted me for a fairly chunky hard-man role – the character was called The Sphinx – but I didn't speak until a lengthy monologue right at the end.

I was told when I was needed, how much I would be earning

and that they would be covering my rent for a place in LA during filming. That was it – my big break in Hollywood.

I'd come from washing pots and pans at a college in Reading, part-time football, humping a black bin liner around with all my worldly possessions – to this.

I nearly fainted when they told me what I'd earn for this. When word got out that I had signed a big-money deal with the man behind *Top Gun* to be in *Gone in 60 Seconds*, it definitely put a few noses out of joint. By rights, out of all of us who had graduated together through those films, I was the one who hadn't worked in the industry before and I guess there was a resentment towards this footballer who had jumped the queue. There was also an element of respect from a lot of actors because they acknowledged what I had done in football, and that I had given a decent account of myself in a completely different field.

So the first big Hollywood film I landed was extra special for a number of reasons.

I had just starred alongside Brad Pitt and Benicio del Toro, which had given me some real confidence, but now I was going to co-star alongside Nicolas Cage, Robert Duvall and a young actress called Angelina Jolie.

I would be lying if I said it wasn't a nerve-racking experience. The audition process, if you could call it that, wasn't exactly the most thorough of experiences, and, even though my confidence was up, I still had the old butterflies going on. All I knew was that my flight to LA and back to meet the director was first class with British Airways, so I felt I had to repay that at least.

Robert Duvall, who I particularly loved in *The Godfather Part II*, was the main man and had a huge aura about him. I made a point of listening and learning everything I could from him when we were on set. I was with him one day when he was telling me how crazy he was about soccer. The conversation moved on to how I had made the move from the game to acting, and that I was reaching a stage where I thought I could get a bit of criticism for only ever playing the hard man. He told me a story that put me at ease, and made me feel about ten foot tall for the rest of filming. He said that John Wayne was a cowboy, and that was what the fans wanted. The point being, there is absolutely nothing wrong with giving the fans what they want. He said, 'Vinnie, your fans want to see you beating people up on the big screen.' It's always stuck with me. Bobby was very good to me on that movie. He asked me to work with him and Ally McCoist on the movie *A Shot at Glory*, but, whichever way I looked at it at the time, I thought I would have been hammered for doing a football film so soon after retiring from the game.

I also really hit it off with Scott Caan, who played a character called Tumbler. He has been in all the *Ocean's* . . . films (*Eleven*, *Twelve* and *Thirteen*) since and made a great living in movies. He was football mad and drove me up the wall asking me about the game and all the old stories. At Warner Bros every lunchtime, we would kick the ball around on the lot.

One day, Scott and the boys and I were playing football by the trailers and Nicolas Cage was sitting on the steps of his, watching us. Then he came out and he tried to have a little game, and he said, 'Hey, man, someone just told me you were a professional soccer player?' I gave him the full Jonah story, and he listened to every word. The Americans are so massive on sport that it gave me a lot of respect from the big hitters.

So my adrenaline was really going on the film and I was

savouring every second of being a Hollywood movie star. I did have a giggle: there were days where it felt like a doddle for me because I was just walking around with my hair shaved with this great costume with people paying a lot of respect to me, and it was a bit different from the early days of my football career at Wimbledon when we'd have a fry-up after training and the old boy cooking would flick fag ash in your eggs.

I was getting on brilliantly with Angelina. I had a lot of time for her and she was a really sweet girl. She was having a lot of problems back then. She was a lot younger and I think she was off the rails for a bit. She was so thin at the time that you could have picked her up with one hand – she was tiny.

I went to a party at her house in Beverly Hills towards the end of shooting. I bumped into a Scottish actor called Tommy Flanagan, from *Braveheart*, there. I was with my new assistant Neil Digweed – he was the old Wimbledon keeper Perry Digweed's cousin (Lorraine had stepped back, wanting to spend more time with her own family) – old mate Graham Coles and one of the actors from *Gone in 60 Seconds*, T. J. Cross.

Angelina's boyfriend at the time, Tim Hutton, had put this bash together and it was really weird. There were some people playing pool and there was a bar in the corner, where I found myself – naturally. It was a collection of people who didn't really know each other. Guys such as Andy Garcia were there, and it was a real introduction to that Hollywood scene. Angelina was walking around in a bathrobe for the whole fucking thing. Her boyfriend suddenly said, in front of all of us, 'If you wanna talk to the Brits all night [meaning me, Tommy and Colesy], we're leaving.' So they left their own party!

When it came to the premiere of the film in Leicester Square I was worried about Angelina. I think by that time she was dating Billy Bob Thornton. He came up to me in LA in a bar one night and said, 'Hey, man. Thanks for being a good friend to my lady.' It was weird. I've got a lovely picture from that premiere in London of us together on the red carpet.

It always struck me how much she loved the Brits. She was married to Jonny Lee Miller for a bit, who I have since worked with, and she was always up for the banter with the British lads and loved our sense of humour. I'm glad it has all come good for her.

I haven't seen Brad and Ange together as a couple in person, but it makes me smile that I worked with them both and they went on to be an item. I spent a great night out with Brad when he was with Jennifer Aniston – it was 2000 at the Oscars' after-show parties and Jen really looked after Tans that night. That was the last big night out we had really.

During the making of that film we managed to rent a place that was up in the Hills, not far from where David Beckham has a place now off Benedict Canyon. It was great, we loved it, and Tans really fell in love with LA. We knew by this point that we really wanted to live in LA full-time.

But I was never sure how long it was going to last at that point and there was still a part of me niggling in the back of my mind that I wanted to give football management a proper spin.

One thing I hadn't achieved was being a successful manager. I had been an assistant with QPR, but never got the chance to pull the strings myself. It was around this time that I started to get involved with Hollywood United, a team of actors and old expat musicians in LA. I just missed being a part of a dressing room, and the only dressing room we had was the beach and the Kings Head in Santa Monica.

I went straight from *Gone in 60 Seconds* to another big-budget blockbuster, *Swordfish*. This time the studio had enough budget for Tans and me to rent a serious mansion in LA. We ended up signing a deal for Bill Withers's house at a real-estate agent's in LA, in the same offices as Larry Flynt. I remember it so well because it was the first time I had set eyes on Larry in that gold wheelchair.

Then I rented a pool table, furniture, everything right down to knives and forks. It was a beautiful place with staff quarters – which came in handy for us because we had so many mates visiting us in LA by this point.

I turned Bill's music studio into a dormitory for all the kids and all their pals with eight single beds up one side and eight up the other side. It had its own door to the pool and it was really snug because it was soundproofed for recording. Jay Statham and Kelly Brook lived with us while he was making his way into Hollywood.

I was sitting in the house one day and Tans said, 'Vin, there's a black guy walking around the swimming pool. What's going on?'

I got my shorts on and went out there and asked this old fella – who was putting some cushions on the lounge chairs – what he was up to. He said, 'Ah, you must be Vinnie? I'm Bill Withers.'

'Lovely day,' I said (echoing the title of his 1977 R&B song). I just couldn't resist it. 'Yeah, heard that once or twice in my time.' And he laughed back.

He had bought some new garden furniture for us and we sat down and got talking. He said he hoped we would have some great memories there with the family and started telling me all about the parties he had held there over the years. We walked up to the tennis court and he said Elvis, the Beach Boys, the Bee Gees – you name anyone in the business – loved coming over to the house for parties. The notorious murderer Charles Manson had even turned up unannounced once, looking for one of the Beach Boys who he had some issue with.

Bill had bought a smaller house on the other side of the hill because he had a smaller family by that time and didn't want to be kicking around a big house. At least that was what he told us. There's a good chance he had hit hard times. That's the way it goes in Hollywood.

But the history was unbelievable and we lived in that house, soaked in Hollywood heritage, for nearly a year. We had our first Hollywood Christmas there and invited Steve Jones from the Sex Pistols, who was also a teammate at Hollywood United. We went to the Beverly Hills Hotel and had a big day out.

It was an amazing neighbourhood. Hemel had a lot of famous footballers in the same area as my house, but in LA we had tennis legend Pete Sampras on one side and model Rachel Hunter on the other.

Sampras got into my limo by mistake that had been sent for me so I could attend a press conference for *Swordfish*. He got a few miles down the road before anyone had realised. His missus came and apologised when I bumped into her at the Four Seasons. We all got on really well – up to a point.

They were getting married in their grounds and I was boasting to Jay Stratham and all the lads that I was going to get the big invite. I've said to Jason, 'Don't worry about that – I'll be getting the call-up from my mate Pete.' This went on for a few weeks and it was getting to the week of the wedding. Sir Elton John was playing the bash and helicopters were everywhere. I was playing tennis with Statham and they were so low that we were firing tennis balls at these photographers up in the sky.

So everyone was asking me if the invite had dropped, and I was giving it the big one: 'Don't you worry! It'll come.' I came home one day, got the letter from the Sampras family, opened it up – boom! I'm thinking, I've got it! I ran up to the house and they were all there looking at me. So I said, 'Here we are, then, Stath. Have a look at this, then!'

I opened it up and read it out: 'Dear Vinnie, we're getting married on Saturday. Can you please turn your sprinklers off at 6 p.m.'

I was gutted. Jay fell about laughing.

So the wedding went ahead, with security everywhere down the perimeter of our house and Pete's. I went through the hedge to security and said, 'Oi, pst! Can you tell Elton it's Vinnie Jones next door. Can you let him know?' I was clutching at straws, promising the girls Elt would get us in. Of course it didn't work. I told Elt about it when I saw him in Australia when I was there promoting *Mean Machine*. He said if he had known, of course, he would have sorted me out. Yeah OK, good one.

It was a really happy time – but I was one decision away from its all being over for good. My inexperience in action movies was to come close to costing me my life, and the Hollywood dream came within a scene of the final curtain. Cue John Travolta – and thank God for stuntmen!

14

John Travolta Saved My Life

I said I went straight to *Swordfish* from *Gone in 60 Seconds*. Well, I remember being linked to a lot of big movies when *Gone in 60 Seconds* was being filmed. A lot of it was really flattering, but I got a bit of a bloody nose when I received a phone call saying I hadn't got the gig on *Gangs of New York*, a massive Martin Scorsese number.

It was my first big rejection in movies. But and old mate of mine from *Snatch*, Stevie Graham, did get the part. I was chuffed for him.

I was gutted and started moping around – but within the hour my manager called and said Dominic Sena wanted me for his next movie *Swordfish* – with John Travolta!

He told me to get down to Universal Studios as soon as possible. I sped off, met with one of John Travolta's 'people', who told me JT had watched *Lock, Stock* and wanted me in *Swordfish*.

Jason Statham had a line in *Snatch*: 'What do I know about dogs?' Well, I was sitting in Universal being offered another big film thinking, Fucking hell! What do I know about movies? I didn't audition, just turned up in a suit. The guy was having three conversations on the phones at once and just told me JT loved me and I had the part. That was it!

It was really good money and I was going to be seriously well looked after.

The role was a decent one, and alongside John Travolta the other stars were Halle Berry and Hugh Jackman.

I had a real moment on that second Hollywood film when I was being driven to work with my former assistant Neil Digweed, the cousin of the old footballer Perry.

We were in Bill Withers's house in the Hollywood Hills by this point and I was chauffeur-driven to work every day, with my first scenes at Frank Sinatra's house!

I walked in and got introduced to everyone. Hugh Jackman was there (great lad) and so was Don Cheadle (another lovely fella). Then Halle comes in. Bear in mind this is a party scene full of extras, and then there's us in this VIP section; there could only have been six of us in that area. She turned every head in the room on her way over to us. As an entrance, it couldn't be beaten.

I have always been conscious not to get too busy when I first find myself in a position like that. Speak when you're spoken to. It was the same thing I had to do with Nicolas Cage on *Gone in 60 Seconds*. When the main guys were all hanging around, I wouldn't really get in among it and try to be a silly bastard with little jokes and stuff.

Anyway, we were waiting and waiting and I could see that even Dominic, the director, was shitting himself.

Then Travolta turned up. It was like Moses parting the Red Sea. He walked in and it was like Elvis on steroids. Everybody was completely silent; you could cut the tension in the room with a knife.

Dominic went up, flapping at him, and Travolta very calmly told him to hold on. He came round the table and shook all of our hands one by one and thanked us for doing the movie with him.

Halle and Hugh were completely cool with it, but you could see the rest of us just visibly go, 'Phew!' It was like a western: he walks in and the music stops; he says something to settle the situation and the music starts again.

He was class. A measure of the man was another gesture he made on the film. I've copied it every time since if I've got a decent lead role.

He came round to all our trailers on the last day of filming and he'd bought us all a Montblanc pen with 'Thanks, JT' on it. On the other side of the pen were the words, 'Swordfish 2001'.

During filming he did something else amazing for me: John Travolta saved my life. Now not a lot of people can say that!

By this stage I had got to know JT quite well and felt comfortable around him. JT had his own trailer and compound – it was the way the big stars would operate, keeping themselves to themselves. I never really understood the etiquette to start with and thought of it as a more expensive caravan park. I would just bowl in there every now and again and say hello. His security looked at me as if I were from another planet. Well, Bedmond was about as far as you could get to this setup. I think he respected the fact that I had played football at a high level and knew I had a certain notoriety back home – so that made the relationship easier to strike up.

Anyhow, we were shooting a big action scene at LAX airport. The scene involved a classic Greyhound coach – a single-decker bus to us Brits. We were doing this bank job and we escaped in the bus before a helicopter flew in, swooped down, hooked chains on us and flew off.

The script explained that we would be flying over downtown LA when the two back wires would break, sending the bus flying backwards on the two chains at the back. I was due to be in the coach looking out and my stunt was pretty dangerous. I was on a wire and I was supposed to fly out the back of the coach, grab one of the hostages on the wire and pull myself up to the helicopter.

So we're on set and they've rigged me up on the wire, full make-up and wardrobe ready for a run-through. The director is getting ready to go and suddenly JT comes in and says, 'Hold on.'

He tugs me aside and says, 'Vin, have you rehearsed any of this?'

I said, 'No, I was just going to do it . . .'

He then insisted, 'No way!'

We were seventy feet up and the ground was concrete below. The only thing I was a bit worried about was the lack of a wide aisle on the bus. It was pretty narrow and the seats were original – normal metal and fabric. They weren't fake prop seats. So I was thinking, I've got to keep my elbows in here. It's gonna smash me up.

JT says, 'No, no, no. I wanna see the stuntman do this before

Vinnie. We'll do it with the stuntman first, *then* Vinnie.'

So my stuntman comes in. He's wearing an identical suit to mine and is kind of like my double. He's harnessed up. They shout, 'Action!' Then they give the direction to break the wires.

The two wires at the back break, the bus lurches down. The stuntman flies back and his safety wire snaps clean off. It's a heart-stopping moment. I can't believe it.

He flies straight through the back of the coach, seventy feet up. There are two actors at the back of the coach. He smashes through them and through the back window and plunges to the concrete floor.

I'm standing by a monitor, watching with the director with my mouth wide open, jaw hitting the floor. Glass goes every-where and we watch him hit the fucking concrete seventy feet below.

We honestly thought he was dead. There was no movement and it was proper panic stations.

Travolta comes running out screaming, 'Give him room! Para-medics!'

Travolta then came over to me when it calmed down a bit and said, 'That's the end of filming today.'

Of course, the guys who set up the stunt were mortified. One guy said to me, 'I've been doing this twenty-five years and this is the first time this has happened to us.'

I'm standing there and I've got adrenaline going now because it has hit me: it could have been me; it could, perhaps should, have been me lying there.

I'd been literally seconds away from doing the stunt. It was only JT's intervention that stopped me doing it.

The stuntman broke his spine. It really smashed him up. He also shattered all the ribs on one of the actors. It was carnage.

The court case went on for years, the actor suing the studio and everything.

When Travolta called it a day on set, I've never seen power like it from an actor. This was at about 11 a.m., so you can imagine what that cost would be to production. It didn't matter. He just said, 'Everyone off set,' and we all went home.

I know it was just that the shock and adrenaline had hit me, but I couldn't control myself.

I caught Hugh Jackman's eye and he was just like, 'Vin! What just happened?!'

Towards the end of *Swordfish*, I was celebrating my birthday at my friend Chris Breed's Cabana Club in LA. I organised a big night out and my assistant Neil said I should invite JT. We got on great but I never thought he would come.

Then all of a sudden, at midnight, in walks JT with his wife Kelly Preston! They came in with a lovely present. Claudia Schiffer was with Matthew Vaughn by then, so she was there too. We sat them all at our table and we all had a dance to the little Irish band we had hired.

That night was when I asked JT about *Pulp Fiction* and he said he went through a dozen pairs of socks in that dance scene with Uma Thurman. All the twisting and shuffling just wore them out.

It was a lovely evening. It was a great honour for me that he showed up. But he didn't just put in a brief appearance: he sat with me and Tans, had a dance with her. There's a lovely picture of me and Tans and JT and Kelly, all of us doing a slow dance.

Months and months later, I got a phone call at the house from John Travolta's PA. They were doing all the press up in Chelsea for *Swordfish*. He invited me up for dinner with Halle and Hugh. I thought it was a really nice gesture. He invited us up for a drink in his suite afterwards, as well.

I became good mates with Hugh. He was a great lad. We used to play cards in my trailer with Don Cheadle. Don was learning his lines for *Ocean's Eleven* at the time. He was struggling with the English accent, so he would spend hours with me just having conversations in English, throwing the old Watford accent back and forth.

It was funny. It was the time before Hugh was a massive star and getting one of the lead parts on *Swordfish* was a good result. These massive Wolverine dolls from *X-Men* had just come out and someone brought one into work. I got it and tied it to my trailer and we used to batter it. Don Cheadle and I used to come past it and we'd be really laying into it. By the end of filming we had mullered it – all the air had gone out of it and it was just a saggy inflatable.

I had a big Union Flag flying from my trailer and one day JT came through, having had lunch with his old *Grease* co-star Olivia Newton-John. He came through in a limo and stopped, and I was sitting having a cigar on the steps of my trailer. The window came down and he said, 'Oh, Vinnie. You know, it's disrespectful to fly your flag without an American flag up as well.'

I said, 'JT, I'm all out of respect today, mate. Don't worry about it.'

He started laughing and as he drove away the black window went up.

He's a top bloke. I was out of respect that day but I've got a lot of respect for JT – and I've got him to thank for my still being on here today.

I was back on track in Hollywood, but back home something really special was brewing.

15

Vinnie Jones, This Is Your Life

Being honoured by *This Is Your Life* on the BBC is one of the greatest moments of my career. It all came about as a complete surprise towards the end of 2000.

Peter Burrell, my manager at the time, had put together a great deal with an energy drink called Red Devil. I had a share in the company and the idea was to build it up with some big advertising campaigns and then sell it on. We had filmed one commercial, which got banned from TV until after the watershed, so there was huge hype about what we were doing. We were going up against Red Bull, but we knew we could kick up a stir and start some momentum.

So Pete phoned me up one day with the news: we had sold the company to Schweppes and the masterplan had worked. A big party was arranged at Café de Paris in Soho to celebrate the handover, so I had to be back in the UK for the press and publicity around it.

I turned up and was doing my bit when Michael Aspel wandered in, came up to me and said the famous words: 'Vinnie Jones, this is your life.'

It just didn't register with me at first. I looked around and thought, Well, there's no one else here and I'm pretty sure he said Vinnie Jones.

It's weird. You can't take it in at first. Then you focus on this big red book and it starts to sink in. I had some friends and family there and the emotions very nearly got the better of me. In all honesty, that was the first time I realised I was a household name in Britain. I realised the football community in the country had a good idea who I was, but suddenly it felt as if everyone from five-year-olds through to ninety-year-olds knew who I was. It was an unusual feeling, but I felt like part of the furniture in the UK.

Filming the show was a great night. It really was something special for me. They whisked me off to the studio and all my suits were already there, lined up by Tans, waiting for me to choose one. I came onto the set to massive applause and it felt like ten times the size of a wedding.

I've got the book on display at home in LA. I've got pictures on the wall in my house with Angelina Jolie, Brad Pitt, John Travolta – but the first thing everybody goes for is that book. It is a great keepsake with all the pictures from that night, about sixty or seventy, of the audience and people walking on. Robert Duvall was on via video link, as were Dennis Wise, John Fashanu, Joe Kinnear, Dave Bassett, Gazza and Frankie Dettori. Guy Ritchie, Jay

Statham and Matthew Vaughn came on together and told some nice stories.

It was a really special night.

In 2004, my dad's brother went to the press and sold his story about when we had a punch up. It was around this time that the *Lock, Stock* family started to split.

Guy had started dating Madonna while he was directing *Snatch*. They had both gone to a dinner as separate guests of Trudie Styler and Sting. They met, clicked and it just snowballed from there. He was on the phone to her all the time during filming.

In 2001, she came to the premiere of another film we all did together – *Mean Machine* – which was actually really cool of her. Sadly, I didn't make it to their wedding. I really wanted to be there but I was filming *Swordfish* and I didn't have the guts to put my foot down on set and say I needed to be elsewhere. It was just too early in my career to throw my weight around like that.

After it had happened, the director, Dominic Sena, came up to me and said, 'Oh, Vin. Your mate's got married. Why didn't you go?'

I said, 'Well, I didn't want to ask!'

He just said, 'Are you crazy? You could have gone. It wouldn't have been a problem.'

I just didn't want to upset the apple cart.

We made up for it at Matthew Vaughn's wedding, though, when he married Claudia Schiffer. I was an usher that day. They'd just bought a house out in Bury St Edmunds and we had a great laugh. It was Jason Flemyng, Jason Statham and I who were the ushers. We were just fucking around the whole time. That was a really good time for all of us.

I remember meeting Claudia for the first time. Matthew came over to LA, called me and said, 'Jones. What are you doing?'

I went, 'We're at home. Do you want something to eat or something?'

He replied, 'Yeah, I'm coming round. I might bring a guest later on.'

Statham and I always used to give Vaughny a hard time, saying his nose would one day be about eight foot long because he told so many porkies.

So, anyway, he came round and he'd got a big smile on his face. I said, 'What's up, Vaughny?'

Tans made him a cup of tea.

He said, 'You'll never guess who I'm dating.'

I went, 'Yeah, go on.'

'Claudia Schiffer,' he beams.

'Fuck off!' I threw all the pillows and cushions at him.

I said, 'Tans. Listen to this lying bastard!'

He said, 'All right, Jones. All right, Jones. I can prove it. I can prove it. It's all hush-hush, but I can prove it.'

So he gets on the phone and goes, 'Darling, darling. Yes, I'm at Vinnie's.'

He gives her the address and, fuck me, half an hour later she turns up!

She had a driver. She'd been doing a job and she'd popped over.

She came in and said hello – and she was so lovely. My mate George Hidge was there with his kids, with his mouth hanging open as she had a cup of tea with us. Fucking hell!

Next thing, she takes all the kids up to the tennis court. She's wearing £20,000 leather boots but just throws them in the corner and starts whacking balls about.

I said to Vaughny, 'Fair play to you, son. She's quality.'

We had a great laugh at the wedding. It was so funny because Statham, Flem and I really wound Vaughny up. When we're together, he gets so nervous. We were telling him, 'We're going to wreck this bloody party tonight, Vaughny. This wedding reception is getting trashed.'

As always, he turned to Flem first, 'Flemyng. You control those two yobs. There shall be no bollocks here tonight. You've got to control those two. It's on you, Flemyng!' Of course Flem's always in on the wind-up. It was a great night and a great wedding.

Mean Machine was the last project we all worked on together in 2001. Matthew came to me and said the words every actor wants to hear: 'I wanna give you your first lead. We'll do *Mean Machine*.'

I think he did it through Ska Films, so Guy was exec producer on it. That was one of the only times I remember being in trouble with them both – when the dog really ran riot. I had gone out until two or three in the morning and missed filming the next day. That was the one and only time I ever did that.

My first leading role, in *Mean Machine*, meant a lot to me. When Robert Duvall had asked me to make a football movie a year or so before, I really didn't want to do it. But this was different. *Mean Machine* was part comedy, part drama, about prisoners playing their guards in a one-off football match. It was an adaptation of the 1974 box office hit *The Longest Yard*.

I insisted the football scenes be realistic. It wouldn't have looked right if proper football people weren't involved to choreograph it and get things right.

So we got my old pal and Crazy Gang ringleader Wally Downes on board. He took trials to grade all the actors on their ability. That was a responsibility he was capable of handling. What he wasn't so competent at was paying the lads on time.

Matthew Vaughn sat him down and explained his responsibilities and then left Wally to draw all the wages for all the players. But, rather than hand them out, he was investing them at the bookies!

So I had all these actors coming to me saying, 'We ain't been paid for three weeks!'

I kicked off with Matthew and asked why. He said: 'They have, we gave it to Wally.'

There were people on the film who wanted to lynch him. He wriggled out of it by sorting all the lads out with some hooky Gucci loafers. I remember him telling the boys, 'Your money's on its way, don't worry about it. It's on the Kempton at two o clock. Go and watch it.'

Adam Fogerty, or Gorgeous George in *Snatch*, was in the film. He was skint at the time, so brought his own one-man caravan to live in on set near Ealing Golf Club. I came back after the weekend and my trailer would be stinking. I eventually worked out that Adam would be going out with Wally and the lads coming back and sleeping in my trailer. It would be stinking of booze, cigars and God knew what – but that's the glamour of the movies!

Mean Machine was the end of a whirlwind for me. The first five movies I had made were an incredible time. *Lock, Stock, Snatch,*

Gone in 60 Seconds, *Swordfish* and *Mean Machine* – it felt as if I had been living life on fast forward.

That run of films was incredible for me and really introduced me to a new world. It made me chuckle, because I was a proper working-class lad but for some reason the toffs absolutely loved me!

And those relationships were to open even more doors for me.

16

The Sound of Music

I've always had really colourful agents looking after my career down the years. It all started off with Eric 'Monster' Hall back in the Crazy Gang days. He was one of the first to cotton onto the whole idea of a footballer having a commercial worth off the pitch.

Later in my playing career, I signed with Jerome Anderson, who made his name representing some of the best players to come out of Arsenal – Ian Wright being his main man.

Around the time this was happening, I had been spending a lot of time with the horseracing crowd. I used to go shooting with a close pal, John Ward, and he told me Frankie Dettori had a great agent.

Frankie and I had become good friends at this point and I knew his man, Peter Burrell, had been with him from when he was a teenager and really guided his career well. John told me Peter was going to be in Barbados on holiday at the same time as I was there with the family. So John set up a meeting and, within five minutes, I was completely bowled over.

His granddad was a very influential geezer in the horse world and I fell in love with him straight away – he was, and still is, an awesome guy. Pete gave me a level of credibility I had been lacking at that point and he made sure I was mixing in the right circles.

I felt like the kids' character Mr Benn – it was as if I had walked through the magic wardrobe into a different outfit on a different planet.

It's hard to put it into perspective without dropping some names. I really have had to pinch myself at certain points in my life: working with Angelina Jolie, Brad Pitt and Robert Duvall; striking up friendships with Ronnie Wood, Rod Stewart, Roger Daltrey and Eric Clapton.

But the one that really got me, through Pete Burrell, was getting close to Sir Anthony and Lady (Carole) Bamford of the JCB digger dynasty. I cast my mind back to the first house I lived in, a shared home on Queens Road in Watford, and here I am hobnobbing with a knighted captain of industry!

We also got pally with Andrew Lloyd Webber and his wife Madeleine, as well as Theo Fennell, the jewellery designer.

They were all really kind to me and Tans. Theo invited us to du Cap for his fiftieth birthday party at Elton John's house.

When we were over there, Lord Lloyd-Webber, Madeleine, Peter, Tanya and I went out for dinner one night. We had enjoyed a few refreshments. We were walking down a cobbled street in du

Taking Nan for afternoon tea with my dad at The Ritz before the *Gone in 60 Seconds* premiere – the only one she was able to attend.

Great mates: me with Angelina on set shooting *Gone in 60 Seconds*.

On the red carpet at Odeon Leicester Square for the premiere of *Gone in 60 Seconds* with Angelina.

Great support from Guy and Madonna at my premiere of *Mean Machine*.

In one of the scenes from *Swordfish* with John Travolta and Hugh Jackman, who I later went on to work with again on X-Men.

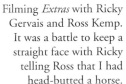

Filming *Extras* with Ricky Gervais and Ross Kemp. It was a battle to keep a straight face with Ricky telling Ross that I had head-butted a horse.

Me as Juggernaut in *X-Men: The Last Stand* – built like a brick shithouse.

Finally getting out of the madhouse during the final of *Celebrity Big Brother* 2010.

Meeting up with Aaron in Watford on his first leave from the Army.

Kaley and Aaron, brother and sister, settling in nicely to life in Hollywood.

Me and Aaron ripping the arse out of it in Bel Air, Hollywood, for lunch (someone's got to do it!)

Keeping in touch with my roots in Hollywood with a 'UK Vin' number plate.

The Hollywood Allstars lads after another trophy winning season.

Me and Tans at the house in Mulholland, ready for a night on the tiles in Beverly Hills.

A normal darts night at my house with not so normal guests – Mark 'Rhino' Smith, Jay and Mickey Rourke

Playing myself in the Hard and Fast campaign for the British Heart Foundation. A bit like Lock Stock, and an overwhelming success. The ad received an unbelievable response and went viral in just two days.

Me, Chris Kamara and Little Vinnie in the second part of the brilliant BHF advert.

My 45th birthday at Hollywood Park Racecourse. A great reminder of what I owe it all to, with a Lock Stock/football cake from the family.

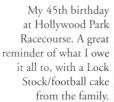

After seeing this picture, I've starting thinking I'm almost there. Sly Stallone, me and Arnie on the set of *The Escape Plan.*

Good mates of mine on the film set, the legend himself Sly Stallone and *The Passion of the Christ* star Jim Caviezel.

Time off the film set with Christian Slater on one of the lakes in Whistler, Canada.

Getting ready for the race of my life in the Arctic Circle for the Discovery Channel.

My new golf mates in Los Angeles: Rob Henderer, the legend that is Joe Pesci and professional golfer David Bergonia.

Flying the flag with Tans at the British Ambassador's House in Los Angeles, 2013.

Cap and I found a little pub with a piano. I shouted, 'Oi, Andy. Let's get in here and have a bit of a singsong.'

The manager was closing the place up but I went over and offered him a few quid to keep it open for a famous musician and some friends.

I said, 'There's ten or twelve of us with Andrew Lloyd Webber. He's going to come in and have a little singsong. How about it?'

The bloke looked Lord Lloyd-Webber up and down, one of the most famous composers of all time, and said, 'No, no, no. Not tonight. No "*sing-song*" – we're closed.'

He then turned his back on us! I just burst out laughing and so did Andrew.

It was Andrew that got the idea of me having a bash at a singing career. The spark for the whole thing was on a night out when Donny Osmond happened to be there. He asked me if I liked to sing and I said, 'When I've had a drink, I'm partial to a singsong. I'll have a bit of "Puppy Love" on the piano if you're game?'

So he got on the piano and everyone was joining in with us.

After he heard my voice, Andrew asked me if I wanted to do the Royal Variety Performance. I thought he was having a laugh! Vinnie Jones singing for the Queen? Life couldn't get more surreal.

He asked me to sing 'Macavity' from *Cats* for the Queen! I couldn't believe what I was hearing, so I mumbled: 'Sing for the Queen? Will she actually be there?'

He said, 'Of course, Vinnie. She will be there, it's her birthday.'

So now the nerves have kicked in and I find myself agreeing to test the old vocal cords a bit more.

The next thing I know, I am having dance classes with the

former *Strictly Come Dancing* judge Arlene Phillips to help with the choreography. The first time we met, she said, 'Right, Vinnie – a footballer, are we? Dancing is a very different type of footwork, but I'll get you in shape.' She came up with a routine with eight backing dancers prowling around me. I've had harder jobs!

When the time eventually came for the Royal Variety Performance at the Lyceum Theatre, I wandered in and found I was sharing a dressing room with Mr Bean! It was unbelievable, Rowan Atkinson – and Stephen Fry – in the same room! I was trying to think of ways I could impress the lads – they are intelligent fellas, after all – when the door was knocked and a runner popped his head in.

He said, 'Vinnie, Elton John would like to have a chat in his suite.'

Brilliant! Good old Elt – he had just given me the best icebreaker ever. So I went upstairs and he had this great big suite. We were having the craic about Watford, football and what was happening with the movies.

After the show you are introduced to the Queen, and you are given a talking-to beforehand with all the 'dos' and 'don'ts'. I just had this thing in my head: 'So what is one going to be doing with one's Cup final tickets this year ma'am?' An old joke from the pub.

Samantha Mumba was waiting in the line-up too. We went on to do a movie together years later called *Johnny Was*. There is a great picture of us in the line-up meeting Her Majesty and shaking her hand. You can tell I've had a couple of glasses of red wine: there's a big grin on Samantha's face as if to say, 'Don't say anything, Vin!'

That performance kicked off a brief spell for Vinnie Jones the pop star.

A mate of mine in the music business arranged for me to record an album of blues and soul songs called *Respect*. When we had it in the bag, I went off and did a one-man show, *An Evening with Vinnie Jones*, all around the UK. We did twelve different shows in fourteen nights. It was brilliant fun going around the country in the tour bus – we packed everywhere out with sixteen hundred to two thousand people every night.

I would sing a couple of songs, then the TV presenter Bradley Walsh would come on and do a question-and-answer session about football, Gazza, right up to the movies. Brad is brilliant at compèring, we go way back, as we played for Rolls Royce years before together – it gave people an insight into me and I made a lot of friends on that tour. Something like four hundred people were queuing up outside to do signing sessions afterwards – I wasn't the wild-eyed midfield hard man any more.

When the album came out in 2002, I did *Top of the Pops* and sang the single 'Bad, Bad Leroy Brown' in the December. I took Kaley with me and she was at that age, around fifteen, where she was trying to be cool about it. When I started singing, I looked out and she was right at the front of the stage with her hands in the air, and she'd forgotten herself, dancing away. That's not her at all, but she just got carried away in the moment – as I did too. It gives me a huge glow to think of that even now.

I really enjoyed the whole experience – the tour, performing in front of a crowd, *Top of the Pops*. I knew deep in my heart that it was the only time I would ever have a crack at being a pop star – so I well and truly enjoyed every minute.

*

The biggest boy band in the country at the time, and probably the world, also came calling. The Westlife lads had had something like nine consecutive number-one singles when I got a call to appear in their new video for the single 'Bop Bop Baby'. I was a bit worried about it at the time because a good run like that has to come to an end at some point, but the lads were fantastic and I thought I would give it a spin. I had met Kian Egan from the band on holiday in Sardinia and we had a great night out. He came along to one of the *An Evening with Vinnie Jones* shows and popped in for drinks afterwards.

They had a treatment for this video with me starring opposite Ronnie Wood's daughter Leah.

Whenever I get a call sheet, I never pay attention to anything else other than the time I need to be out of my bed and into the car. I never really look at where we're actually filming. It's still the same now when I'm filming.

I've talked a lot about fate, destiny, premonitions and pure coincidences in this book so far – well check this one out. The car I'm in pulls up to the location in Watford for the shoot – the International University of Europe in Bushey, where I was a groundsman! It was the place where I kicked a football again for the first time in three years with Wealdstone after I'd packed it all in after leaving home. I used to cut the grass and weed the flower displays and here I was, as a paid actor, doing a video with Westlife!

It was a really brilliant video – but, typically, it was the first one not to get to number one.

I had a great craic with the lads, though, and we were filming for a few days together. I had ordered a new car and decided, to be a bit flash and show the young lads how it was done, to get the garage to deliver the car to the shoot.

It actually meant a bit more to me than that: it was a symbolic thing. When I'd last worked there, I was on £50 a week and wearing rotten green overalls. Suddenly, here I was getting a brand-spanking-new Bentley delivered to the same spot. It was surreal.

So the car shows up while we're filming a scene where I arrive on a horse into this chapel. The next thing, a runner comes over and tells me the Bentley is here. They have taken it off the trailer and made the brilliant decision to hand the keys to Brian McFadden. Of all the people.

The director has shouted, 'Cut!' and I go running round the corner to see my new motor.

The first thing I see is Brian flying out towards the road in my new car, sticking his fingers up out the window. Off he goes, straight out into the main road. God knows if he had a licence, let alone insurance at that point. He looked like he was only about seventeen. Luckily for me, and him, there were no bumps or scrapes when he came screaming back into the car park. I suppose I got my own back by ending their run of number ones!

Pete Burrell had opened a door to another world for me by this point.

We were invited everywhere, including being guests of honour in Dubai for the World Cup horse meeting. We had a seven-thousand-square-foot room, first-class flights. I honestly couldn't believe what was happening to us – and still can't.

Peter was the best for horseracing. He sorted a trip to Cheltenham another time and, for some reason, I couldn't get there in time. No problem: Sir Anthony Bamford sent the helicopter for me. The official JCB chopper! I had a mate, Pat Curtin, with me and we jumped out of the chopper – and they had a Land Rover that drove us straight up to the JCB box. We stood on their balcony and watched the whole of the meet from there. If you had told me that would happen to me when I was drinking in Bedmond as a young man, I would have laughed at you. Vinnie Jones on the champagne, on a balcony at Cheltenham.

But it wasn't just me who tasted the generosity of the Bamfords. At another party, I was telling them about my son, Aaron. At the time Aaron was obsessed with diggers, tractors, Tonka trucks and JCBs. A few weeks later, Pete called me and said, 'Anthony and Carol want to take Aaron to the factory where they build all the JCBs.' They sent the helicopter to Elstree to pick up Aaron. He flew to the factory and had the full red-carpet treatment. Ten years on, Aaron still talks about it. He's still got all the toys Anthony gave him that day.

I was always concerned the Bamfords would be put off by the reputation I had through football for not being afraid of a bit of fisticuffs. Oddly enough, I helped them out on an occasion on that front.

We were in Barbados with them and their son Joe. They threw this amazing party and I did my usual trick of inviting about half the people we met at the hotel. We had six tickets and turned up at the door with about twenty-five people. As you might have gathered, the Bamfords are a generous bunch and didn't bat an eyelid.

We had been in there for a while when Carol Bamford came

running through in a rage about some Rastafarian lads out the back who were dealing drugs at the back gate. The local security lads didn't look as if they fancied it at all, so I said, 'Lady B, what's the matter?'

She explained, so I headed down the garden and out the little wooden door on to the beach. I went out there, shut the door behind me – no one knew I'd gone – and I had a tear-up with the pair of these big Rastas.

There was a bit of a commotion and the doors opened with people spilling out to see what was happening. It was the end of the punch-up. I had sent them packing and I came back in for another drink. Lady Bamford said, 'Oh, you saved the day Vinnie!'

The next day, they sent round this massive slab of caviar to us at the hotel – and we still get a Christmas card from them to this day.

Sadly, my next punch-up didn't end so nicely. Just with a life-time ban from Richard Branson's airline.

17

Air Rage and Air Miles

I haven't been welcome on a Virgin Atlantic flight for well over ten years now, as I write this. There is a lifetime ban in place, which is a shame really: I spend a lot of money flying back and forth between London and LA, and they are missing out on the business. Maybe one day we'll make peace.

It all boils down to another classic episode in my life of the dog getting the better of me, fuelled by a few too many drinks. I was flying from Heathrow to Tokyo in May 2003 when it all kicked off again. This time, it was in the upper class cabin on a Virgin Atlantic long-haul flight where they have a little bar so you can split the journey up and have a few drinks. The row started when some passengers told us to pipe down. As always in my case, a few drinks too many ended up with a full-scale shouting match and a bit of a grapple with a bloke on the flight.

It cost me £1,100 in fines, costs and compensation for 'air rage' offences as well as another heavy stint of a hundred and eighty hours' community service.

The truth is, I regret the whole ugly episode – and held my hands up in the end. When I hear that line about my telling the stewardess, 'I can get you murdered; I can get the whole crew murdered for three thousand pounds,' it makes me shiver. The fact is, I don't recall saying that. The dog had taken hold of me. The staff on the plane said in court that I had 'intimidated' them. I sometimes forget that I can come across that way. It was like the trip to Ireland when I bit the reporter's nose – it might be behaviour I would get away with in the company of my old mates in Bedmond, but not on a plane. And not in front of loads of passengers. I formally apologised to the cabin crew. In total, it was a £500 fine, £300 costs and £300 compensation. The prosecution lawyers withdrew a charge of being drunk on board an aircraft – which had a maximum of two years inside as punishment.

We were living between LA and Tring, Hertfordshire, at the time and it caused a lot of hassle for me with my travelling. It was my own fault, and the bloody dog's, and it made me buck up my ideas for a long time. It wasn't the last time I would appear in court over a brawl, but the episode in the years to come, a bit later in this book, was a lot more damaging physically and financially.

I had been making the flight to Tokyo to go the long way round to Hawaii on a film, *Big Bounce*, with Owen Wilson, Morgan Freeman and Charlie Sheen. It's mad to think the way Charlie is now compared with how he was back then – if anything *I* was the bad boy after the Virgin incident. He was clean, like a little saint, back then as far as I was aware.

Owen Wilson is fanatical about sport and if we weren't filming he would have us up at his house with every game possible going. You name it, he had it – with all the remote controls at hand to keep up to date. I always remember going up there. He had a big island in his kitchen full of scripts. It was unbelievable – and a reminder of my place in the pecking order.

We stayed in the hotel where *Forgetting Sarah Marshall* was filmed, starring Russell Brand. We all had tennis courts at the back of our rooms, with the front overlooking the ocean. Owen was nuts on his football, so we used to play head tennis, two versus two, with Morgan Freeman watching us as an independent umpire! He used to love it, sitting there with his pipe, laughing at our banter.

Charlie had been a really talented baseball player in his day. He got the boys together one afternoon and got us on the beach for a game of softball. He kept himself to himself during filming, so it was quite unusual for him to organise something for us all.

He was just whacking this ball for miles; it was seriously impressive. Then he said, 'Come on, Vin. Have a go.' I thought, being a decent sportsman and a handy golfer, I would be all right. I thought I'd smash it straight over their heads – but it was nigh on impossible. I couldn't hit the bloody thing and it was embarrassing! We had such a laugh, though. So much for the professional sportsman!

I haven't seen Charlie for a while, and I'm sure I won't for a while, given the state he's in.

I had a really busy couple of years around then, going from film to film. I had a big part in a comedy caper called *EuroTrip*, playing

Mad Maynard, a bloke a bit like the Vinnie Jones you might have found in Bedmond if you had gone looking for me in the early eighties.

I played my part in eleven films over a three-year period, starting with *Night at the Golden Eagle* with James Caan. I went on to *Big Bounce* with Charlie after that, then a movie called *Blast* with Eddie Griffin and Shaggy. *Slipstream* came after that with Sean Astin, who went on to star in the *Lord of the Rings* trilogy as Samwise Gamgee.

I joined up with my old *Lock, Stock* mate P. H. Moriarty in a movie called *The Riddle* after that, with another big action hero, Steven Seagal. From there I got to share the screen with a true thespian, Patrick Stewart, a great British actor, in *Mysterious Island*. I once had a conversation with Michael Caine about making certain movies for money. He said that for every *Get Carter*, *Zulu*, *Italian Job* or *Alfie* there would be one *Jaws 4* to pay the bills. That's the way I look at a lot of the movies I have made. You know from the very start if something is going straight to DVD – but that's a decision you have to make as a husband and a father. I still have bills to pay and I had a mortgage for a long time. That's the way of the world. I have made a lot of movies; some of them have only been released in Kazakhstan, but they paid for the cabana, and I can live with that.

It was a spell in my life that paid for our house on Mulholland, the gaff next to Quentin Tarantino. It has been a big job getting it into the shape we wanted, and a lot of Mexican builders have done very well out of it! I realised I had done all right when the Hollywood tour buses started passing our house. They would get out and take their pictures, and I would see them on our CCTV cameras. Just as they got back in the bus, I would press the button to open the gates. Then they would all get out again waiting with their cameras, I'd leave it a couple of minutes, and close them again. It's just a bit of mischief – the kind of nonsense I would be getting up to if I was still in football.

I did some serious travelling and racked up enough air miles over that period to keep me in flights for a lifetime. One of the most arduous journeys I had was Hawaii to Heathrow, then on to South Africa. I was in the air for thirty-six hours, then there was all the time spent with connections. That said, ask me to swap back to getting up at 6 a.m. in the winter to go and dig out some foundations, and I would take the flying any day of the week! Before you do it, you imagine the travelling to be a really glamorous side of the business, but the truth is it can be draining – and occasionally, terrifying.

I had one really big scare when I was going to Australia to film *The Condemned* with Stone Cold Steve Austin. It was a movie financed by World Wrestling Entertainment, or WWE.

There was a geezer next to me on the flight from LA who was a bit of a miserable fucker. After my own slip-up on a flight, I'm sensitised to someone being a bit rude, and he was really chippy with the steward. It is a lesson in being careful what you wish for, because I was looking at him thinking, Miserable bastard. If something happened to this plane now, if we have a crash, that would be the last thing the poor bloke would remember. He's on his laptop computer and the plane has just gone into a vertical nosedive.

We're in a 747, a jumbo jet, and it has wobbled – then plunged into a dive. His stuff's gone everywhere and he's ended up on the floor, under two seats. This is before they could even say, 'Fasten seatbelts.' I've just grabbed my seatbelt and somehow put it on. First Class is empty and I am seriously thinking, This is it. Game over.

All sorts are going through my head. Do I get my phone out and try to call Tans? What about Aaron and Kaley?

The steward bloke is on the floor too, absolutely terrified, his eyes wide open. And people can't even scream because the dive is so hairy. All of a sudden the plane pulls up and levels off, with G-force.

I looked over at the guy who was being rude earlier and he'd wet himself. I looked at him just about long enough for him to know I had noticed, then sorted my stuff out that had gone flying. It was genuinely terrifying. The whole place was covered in spilled drinks.

I spoke to the steward and he said it was his sixteenth year and that was the worst experience he had suffered in a plane. It seemed like twenty seconds, maybe more, at 500 m.p.h. We never got an explanation, but we were told there was an investigation into it. I thought it must have been to deliberately avoid another plane. I was just thanking my lucky stars I was alive.

Once I came back from Australia, I had a TV job in England that I thought would be a little cameo and nothing more. I signed up to film *Extras* with Ricky Gervais and Ross Kemp. The show turned out to be a massive success off the back of *The Office*. I really hope he brings it back – I would fancy a regular slot alongside his *Office* character David Brent. I got on like a house on fire with Ricky, talking football and having the craic.

I was supposed to walk into our scene, giving it the classic

Vinnie anger. I couldn't do it. I kept looking at him and he said something about 'headbutting a horse'. He came out with all these one-liners and it took me about three or four takes to get it right because every time I looked at that silly little grin of his I was bursting out with laughter. It's amazing how people still come up and talk about that show. I was over a third of the way into my movie career by that point, and the power of TV in the UK really hit me. It's the same in the US now.

My film career was about to get another massive boost, with one of the biggest parts I had secured in Hollywood to date.

I took a call from my old pal Matthew Vaughn, inviting me up to his office in Beverly Hills for a chat about a new action movie he was working on. He said, 'Jones, I've just read this *X-Men* script for the first time and there's a character called Juggernaut – I think you are my man.' So I went up to see him and the production staff had prepared an incredible series of story boards, with all the characters illustrated for him to get an idea of the film. He said, 'I thought they'd drawn a picture of you, Jones. Check him out – big chap.'

Matthew introduced me to the producers and I basically got the job there and then – it was all down to my old mucker from *Lock, Stock.* It all felt as if it was signed and sealed until I got another call, this time with less positive news.

It was Matthew again, about a month later. He said, 'Vin, have you signed your contract for *X-Men*?'

I said, 'I'm not sure. I left it all to my agent.'

He replied, 'Look, I'm just tipping you off. I'm walking off the movie tomorrow because I'm not happy with how long we've got to prep it and everything else. So I don't want to be held responsible if it doesn't happen.' I thought it was *Gangs of New York* all over again – a rejection was in the post. I knew there was something else in the pipeline, *Stardust*, and Matthew wanted to cast me in that too, but it wasn't a concrete offer. He thought I was in danger, along with all the other people he brought into *X-Men*, of being recast.

I was up in Canada making a movie, so I couldn't get to LA to sign a contract in person and I was in a panic. I was walking through reception when this really bubbly, bouncy guy rocks up to me. It was the first time I had set eyes on the fella and he says, 'Vinnie. I'm a big fan of yours.' I was like, 'Oh, hello, mate.'

This guy had an impressive entourage following him along. It was Brett Ratner, the new director of *X-Men*. He said, 'You're my man for Juggernaut. You tell that Guy Ritchie you're doing all my movies now, and no more for him!'

It was a real thank-God-for-that moment. I actually signed for *X-Men: The Last Stand*, the third in the *X-Men* series, and for the next movie and the next movie after that. That's how long they tie you in for on a huge franchise like that. That was an unbelievable time. They had to make me up to be this massive character who could run through walls, so I was flying backwards and forwards for hours of prosthetics. I was living in England around that time while the kids finished school, but found myself making return trips to LA for costume fittings, first-class on British Airways.

When it actually came to filming, we had the biggest base camp of any movie I had ever worked on. It was an incredible sight. On the big movies before that, all the main actors would segregate themselves from the rest of the cast with their own catering and supporting team.

On the *X-Men* movies I made sure I had an open door and made my trailer the centre of activity. There was a lovely old lad from the East End of London who had done all the big movies, Denis Brock. He was the head lighting boy and he had a few other English lads working as grips. They were all really into their football, so I made sure I had big screens on and arranged sandwiches and beer for all of us. It was like a youth or a social club at times. The Union Flag I had flying on that trailer is the one that now hangs outside my gaff in LA.

About five years before the film started shooting I had worked with Hugh Jackman on *Swordfish*. He was the main character, Wolverine, in *X-Men*, but he seemed as if he had changed over the years.

When we made *Swordfish* I regarded him as a close mate. He had been in hysterics when we battered his Wolverine inflatable on set – I remember him telling the ex-boxer Oscar De La Hoya about it when we were out one night. I thought he would have been inviting me out for dinner to catch up and that nothing would have changed.

It was strange. They got me up to Canada to rehearse fight scenes with him and I thought it would be like old times. He was there with his missus and I was giving it the usual carry-on – and he wasn't really warming to it at all. He was very matter-of-fact, professional and precise about what I would be doing with the stuntmen rather than him, and it felt like his guard was up. He was nice enough, don't get me wrong. I don't know if it was me, or other people telling him to keep himself to himself.

When we started filming I rented a house and got the whole family up there. It was a blessing because Statham was doing a movie in Vancouver too, so I had a mate nearby and Tans staying with me the whole time.

In the end, the process of making the movie was enjoyable on the whole. I vowed never to do a movie that required so much time in Makeup again – but that went out the window a few years later.

X-Men 3, as it's often called, came out and was a huge box office hit despite a few dodgy reviews. It made something like $460 million worldwide, the most financially successful of the series at that point.

It catapulted me onto a whole new level of recognition in America – something I wasn't quite prepared for. When it did really hit home, I would be waking up handcuffed to a hospital bed fearing I was blind.

18

Sioux Falls Nightmare

Since I was a kid, I've had a great love for the outdoors. If my cards in life had fallen differently, I still believe I would be working as a gamekeeper – and loving every second of it. I still get the same buzz from going shooting with some of the boys as I did when I was growing up. I don't get out as much as I used to when we had the house in the Hertfordshire countryside, but I still do go away on trips with the lads when it fits in with filming and commitments I have in LA.

In 2008, some of the guys I know out here, one who owns restaurants and a few of our shared friends, decided to go on a pheasant shoot. We flew down to South Dakota in early December. There was snow on the ground there and it was a nice change from the LA sunshine.

After a day outdoors, we were on our way back to the hotel and decided to stop for a drink and something to eat in a place called Sioux Falls – not the biggest town in the world but it looked like a reasonable place.

As we walked in, I saw a group of lads at the bar going backwards and forwards to the pool tables with drinks. I remember thinking, I'll steer clear of them and keep my head down. I had done a few pictures with some girls in the bar who had clocked me – I had done *X-Men: The Last Stand* around then, so they recognised my face.

The mood wasn't so bad, so we had a drink and I thought I'd have a game of pool with the lads I was with. So I went over to chalk my name on the board. I walked over and this geezer stood right in front of me.

He went, 'What you doing?'

I said, 'Just having a game.'

He said something to me about *X-Men* and being the big tough man, which I didn't quite catch. I didn't pay any attention to it, just tried not to get drawn in.

Then he pointed at my head and asked: 'What hat is that?'

I had a black LA Dodgers hat on. As I turned the hat round, the geezer behind him just spat in my face. As he spat I put my arm out in front of me. Matey boy, who started this, was holding a big old stein in his hand, one of the big heavy ones. My arm was already out so I couldn't even put my hand in front of my face when he suddenly crashed the glass into my face, full force. It sent me back, stumbling on my feet. By now, another one of his mates had come round on the other side. As I went back, this mate crashed a Budweiser bottle on the back of my head.

Down I went. As I fell, I heard this girl screaming, 'He's got a knife! He's got a knife!'

I just went to roll up into a ball.

You would think someone had cut my throat. The amount of blood was ridiculous. I could hardly see anything. Looking back on it, I think I was probably concussed, but the blood was in my eyes and I couldn't see, which made matters even worse.

By the time I got up, the big fella – Juan Barrera his name was – had scarpered. The manager had come over and a girl appeared with a towel. They said I had to go. She was screaming, 'Oh my God, it's bad, it's bad.' I didn't feel pain, it was just the blood I was worried about. I remember thinking, Shit! What damage has he done? I was worried about my eyes – I couldn't see because there was so much claret.

The big fella Barrera – he must have been well over 300 pounds, which is over 21 stone – had left the bar by a side door. It connected through to the toilets. The manager took me the same way, with the girl holding the towel against my face to stop the bleeding.

As we got into the corridor, I was suddenly facing up to this Barrera guy again. As I took the towel away from my face I could see he had another tumbler, a glass, in his hand. I just reacted straight away. I totally lost it. I threw a couple of punches at him. He grabbed hold of me and spun me round and everyone jumped in and pulled us apart. When he threw me, I was like a rag doll – and I'm a big, 215-pound bloke. He just tossed me to the ground. One of the lads I had been hunting with was by my side at this point and he somehow spun Barrera round. It really kicked off.

The *Sun* newspaper got hold of the CCTV footage a few weeks later. I could hardly bring myself to watch it.

After the clash in the corridor, the manager pushed me out of a door. He was shouting, 'Get out. Get out quick.'

All I remember was being in the snow. It was freezing and I could see my red blood dripping into the perfect white snow. I was looking round and didn't have a clue what was going on. I picked up a lump of snow in the tea towel and put it against my face. I sort of popped my tongue out to check my teeth and lips and I could feel something resting against my upper lip. I took one hand off the towel to see what it was. It was my nose, hanging off and resting against my top lip.

I knew I was in real trouble at that point. The whole of my nose was cut in half, hanging off my face. You could have put an old 50p piece in the hole I could feel above the gap. I couldn't believe it. That was when I really started to worry. Not again, I thought.

I could feel most of the bleeding to the left-hand side of my face. I went to move the ice pack to the other side and, as I moved, I felt my left ear touching my chin – it was hanging by a thread as well.

The thoughts were now swirling: I really am in big trouble here; it can't get much worse.

One of the boys came running out and said, 'We've got to get you to hospital, Vin. This is bad.'

I can't remember how but they did get me to a hospital. I could see that the doctors and nurses were shocked by it – they were all panicking. So I could tell it was bad from their reaction. Anyway, the doctor came in and said he could stitch the side where my ear was ripped off back up. I also had a big gap on my forehead where the glass must have smashed and, as he was checking me out, he said he was going to have to call the plastic surgeon – it was that serious.

By now, the shock had well and truly sunk in. I was shaking. My whole body was out of control.

About an hour later, the plastic surgeon came in. He gave me a shot and I faded off to sleep under general anaesthetic. I woke up a bit later and the lad Owen, who we were shooting with, was lying in the chair. He had stayed with me all the way through it.

I remember croaking: 'Owe, how is it, son?'

He just looked at me with this look on his face and said: 'It's sixty-eight stitches, Vin. The plastic surgeon's been working on you for hours.'

I was scared at that point. I hadn't seen my face and feared the worst.

Explaining the fight, Owen said, 'It happened so quickly, none of us could react. We couldn't get in to help you out and they all bolted.'

When a nurse finally came in with a mirror, I looked like a mummy. I was all bandaged up. I just thought, Jesus Christ, you've done it this time. Owen said to me he couldn't believe I hadn't lost my eyes.

So, anyway, I wanted to get out of there before the local press got on to it.

In the morning at about eight, the nurse came in and told me I had to ring this number. It was the local sheriff, a copper. She said he wanted to take a statement as soon as possible. I thought, Great, they're gonna nick them.

So I called the copper and they came within five minutes. He came in, turned me round and stuck the handcuffs straight on.

I said, 'What are you doing?'

He replied, 'I am arresting you for assault.'

I was absolutely gobsmacked.

He said, 'Mr Barrera is pressing charges. He said you attacked him on the way to the toilets.'

I said, 'You are having a laugh! Tell me you are having a laugh. You are joking.'

He took me down to the station, put me in a cell and left me there for a bit. Then he came back in and took my statement. The next thing I heard was that they had arrested the first geezer who'd glassed me.

Again, I thought that was good news and that it wouldn't be long before the whole misunderstanding was put to bed and the true culprits were found guilty. Then I got the news that they had released the other fella without charge. I had to give them $800 to bail myself out. It really was going from bad to worse.

Next thing, I was sent a charge sheet. Three charges of assault on Mr Barrera. Charges dropped against all the others. The nightmare was just getting worse.

So I flew back to LA, got out of Burbank Airport, and it was an absolute circus with the media. Everyone was there – TV cameras, press. Tans was there, too. She was shaking and crying.

We jumped into the car and I explained everything to her again, as I had done on the phone. She was looking at my face and I could tell she was really upset and worried. We've been through everything together over the years and here we were again, dealing with something I thought was a drama that would die down in a few weeks. I couldn't have been more wrong.

I got a court date and had to employ a local attorney. They don't like it if you get an outsider coming in.

A couple of months later, I flew back to Sioux Falls and appeared in court in front of a jury to face the charges. During that time, they had raided Barrera, who was the one pressing charges, and found a load of guns, knives and drugs. Everything. So he was a star witness.

I went into court and it turned out he was the prosecution's *only* witness. They called Barrera and he came out in an orange prison suit, shackled around the ankles and wrists. Two armed coppers brought him in. It was an absolute farce. A total shambles.

Anyway, the jury went out and deliberated for about twenty minutes and then we were called back in. I was confident justice would prevail, but my heart was in my mouth nonetheless.

First count of assault: 'Not guilty.' Second count of assault: 'Not guilty.' Third count of assault: 'Not guilty.'

I came out of the court feeling as though a huge weight had been lifted. I knew I was completely innocent, but it is never a good feeling being in the hands of a jury in a place so far from home. I needn't have thought like that, though. As I walked out of the court, members of the jury came up to me and said, 'We're so sorry this happened in our town. Please don't think badly about where we come from. It's not a true reflection of the town or this area.'

At one point before the trial, it was suggested that I plead 'no contest'. There was no danger that I was prepared for compromise. I was completely innocent and refused to accept anything less.

Despite knowing I wasn't in the wrong, I honestly thought it was shaping up to be the end of my Hollywood dream. It was like history repeating itself – things going well and then something coming along out of the blue to trip me up. The house we have up in Mulholland was set up and we were settled in. The roots were down and we couldn't have been happier. Then this.

Flying back from the trial was a total relief. I had a week of the press flying around and sitting outside my house waiting to get a question in. I spoke to a friend of mine at the *Sun* and we talked the story through at every stage, from the moment I got out of hospital to the actual trial. I was glad I could explain the truth to everyone back home.

The heat from that incident eventually wore off, but I still had to deal with more legal problems, which were not resolved till the beginning of 2013.

At the time of the court case, an oily little weasel of a geezer in a cheap grey suit bowled up to me and tried to put a letter in my hand, serving legal papers, shouting, 'Mr Jones. Have that!' My lawyer stepped in the way and spun the geezer round saying it wasn't the time or the place.

My brief opened the letter and it was from the lawyers acting on behalf of the other guy who glassed me. According to the letter, he had cut his arm during the fight and he was proceeding with civil litigation! My lawyer read it to me and I couldn't believe what I was hearing. He was suing for loss of earnings because of *his* injuries.

I asked my legal advisers what I should do and they said I should countersue for loss of earnings, too.

Next thing, I got a call from my lawyer saying this guy's representatives had been on the blower and said they would be happy to settle for $350,000!

I was livid. I told them to ring back and say I wouldn't settle. We were going all the way on this. So, anyway, time went by, and we found out his lawyer was from Texas and had read about the case, then done a bit of ambulance-chasing hundreds of miles away and maybe he had promised to fight the case on a 'no win, no fee' basis on the proviso they would split any money they got out of me.

As if that weren't enough, Barrera also tried to sue me through the civil courts. He wanted $25,000 and, while he was still in prison, I settled for $10,000. I needed it to all go away, and not spend the rest of my life shelling out for legal bills. My costs were $60,000 in total on the civil front. It was at least $40,000 to fight the criminal case, when all costs were taken in. That's not to mention the 68 stitches and being scarred for life.

I might have got the 'not guilty' verdicts, but, while that was outstanding, I had to go into Customs and Immigration in the US every time I flew into the country. I would be queued up with all the villains in secondary passport control whenever I came back into the country. It was another three hours going through your papers and they really interrogate you.

The whole saga had been a real pain in the arse, but looking back on it, I think I was so lucky I never lost my sight. The other civil case was dismissed, rightly so.

It also made me realise how lucky I was to have CCTV evidence in the case. During the trial, they showed the whole thing.

It proved beyond any doubt that they had started the fight and attacked me. It also showed Barrera cocking his arm in the corridor as if he was preparing to hit me and have another go at me.

I called the plastic surgeon in 2012 to say thanks for working his magic on me. I sent a massive bunch of roses to the nurses in the hospital not long after it happened too. The authorities wanted to send me my bail money back, but I told them to give it to a local charity.

I've been in some scraps in my time, but that one could have blinded me. In fact, it could have been worse than that: I could have been killed.

Not even John Travolta could have saved me from that one.

They say it never rains, but it pours. I would have taken one of Mother Nature's tamer elements rather than the next incident, which would shake my life to the core.

19

Big Brother, Big Bother

What better way to get over a potentially life-threatening incident than getting yourself involved in another one?

This time an earthquake clocking 5.4 on the Richter scale was the biggest reminder of my mortality – and in an office block fourteen floors up, where I was auditioning to appear in *Hell Ride*. The irony of the title of the film and the events wasn't lost on me – another example of what I mentioned right at the start of this book.

I had never experienced an earthquake before that day in 2008. I could feel the building start to sway; I looked out of the window over LA and the whole place was shaking like something from a disaster movie. It was a strange feeling when it kicked off: I felt a bit seasick and it made my legs go a bit wobbly. I didn't know if I should run for the door or just keep staring out of the window.

If the tower block had come down that would have been it for me. Everything seemed to survive, miraculously, but I was straight on the phone to Tans to check she was OK, and everyone in LA just got back to normal – bar the odd change of under-pants.

I got the part – playing Billy Wings opposite David Carradine, Dennis Hopper and Michael Madsen – and I was cast by my neighbour Quentin Tarantino, who was one of the producers.

I had started auditioning most of my parts in an American accent around that time but *Hell Ride* was my first real effort in full American and my confidence was up afterwards. I was asked in to audition for *Year One*, a big $60 million movie starring Jack Black and Michael Cera.

Pete Burrell had started to take more of a back seat as my agent by this point, handing everything over to Alex Cole in LA, who had been managing me for a few years in the US. And it was Alex who had arranged for me to do a reading after a few more dia-logue lessons with a guy who helped Hugh Jackman crack a decent American accent. I wanted to make an impression and land the part.

So I turned up for this session and there was an older bloke with grey hair and glasses who looked quite familiar. They intro-duced him as 'Harold' and the penny dropped – Harold Ramis. His film *Caddyshack* was a favourite of the Crazy Gang, and if the lads had known I was in the same room as he was they would have exploded!

I had to settle myself down very quickly and deliver a threat, in my best American accent, to the guy I was reading with. So I did my bit reasonably well, I have to say, and that was me for the day.

Two weeks later I got a call to say I had landed the part – four months in New Orleans, all expenses paid, for me and Tans!

When we got down there I had a run-through of the script with all the other cast members, which is a nerve-racking experience. My mate Harold was there and I asked him how he wanted me to speak in the movie. I said, 'Shall I do it in my American accent from the reading, or English?'

He said, 'Oh, no. Just do it exactly how you did it in the audition, in English.' That had been my best American accent and he thought it was my English! A little reminder of my limitations.

I dipped my toe in Ross Kemp territory by doing a TV series called *Toughest Cops* after that. I narrated the first series and it went really well, so they commissioned me to get in among the muck and bullets and actually go on patrol around the world.

At one point, we were in New Orleans and we were following this kid on a bike who was looking a bit suspicious. Suddenly, he just threw this package into the bushes and tried to bolt. The squad car caught him, no problem, and got him in the back while we found the package. We unwrapped it and found a loaded Glock! This lad must have been in his early teens, and he was carrying a deadly weapon. When the cops asked him why he had it, he came out with a story that I wouldn't even have dared to use back in the Bushey days! He said he had chased a chicken under a house and found it, then came out to dispose of it and we caught him doing that. It was incredible.

Then we went to Baltimore, where the hit series *The Wire* was based, and that was a real eye-opener. We had a car chase with a young guy in a pickup. He made a good go of a getaway, but eventually he was caught. Not long afterwards, we were called out in the squad car to a fight at a house nearby and it was the same kid, with an older guy knocking seven bells out of him. I've seen some fights in my time but this guy was really getting a beating. It turns out it was a father and son, and the son had stolen his dad's car to sell because he was a raging heroin addict and needed the cash. I spoke to the young guy and he said he just couldn't help himself – he was hopelessly addicted to drugs. It stuck with me because he was younger than Spud, my Aaron. We are so lucky our two kids have turned out so well.

Toughest Cops was another life-changing experience, seeing what some of the cops around the world have to deal with – more trouble than I am when I've had a few beers, that's for sure. It was a great experience and a very successful show.

I did a few voiceovers for big animated movies, too – *Madagascar* and *Garfield.* They are great work if you can land them. You've got all the dialogue there in front of you, so you're not up all night learning it. I got a smallish fee for *Garfield* but I get massive residuals year after year. *Madagascar* took $400 million worldwide, so I should be able to pay my golf membership for years to come. You get about $15,000 to $20,000 for a couple of days' work, but residuals in the first year with that success can add up to $100,000. You could get that for two or three years, every year, then it goes down and down but it's still a nice little windfall every year.

I had a good run for a couple of years when I was working constantly, and I hardly had time to pull my boots on for Hollywood All Stars.

I had a joint leading role with Bradley Cooper on *The Midnight Meat Train*, a thriller. Another name that went on to do pretty well for himself after brushing shoulders with the old

VJ! Three more films, *The Heavy*, *The Bleeding* and *Assault of Darkness*, all came out in 2009, as well as an appearance on the chat show of my old *News of the World* boss: *Piers Morgan's Life Stories*.

In all honesty, it was only around that time that I really drew the line under making a return to football. I have never said it before, but up until that point, had Ken Bates called me up and asked me to manage Leeds United, I would have said yes.

Some people might think I had been out of the game too long, but the fact is, Leeds were in real trouble and what they needed was a character to come in and give them some backbone. I thought a lot I had learned in Hollywood would serve me well in the game. I certainly know how to deal with agents and big egos! That being said, the football side of it never leaves you. You just need some strengths to cover your weaknesses and that's where guys like Don Howe have always excelled.

The reality of it now is that I couldn't afford it. It sounds like a lot, but being a manager on two or three grand a week would be a massive step back. It's not so much the money: we've got such a nice lifestyle in LA with the golf and the weather. I always believed in the mantra 'Never say never', but I think I actually shut the door on professional football for good at that point in my life.

Shortly after I appeared with Piers on ITV, I got a call through my agent Alex Cole, saying *Celebrity Big Brother* wanted me to appear in the 2010 show. The producers had put together an incredible offer, which they sold to me as 'the million-dollar man'. Their plan was for me and Gazza to go on the show together, as old pals, and split a million-dollar fee. I couldn't get hold of Gazza at the time – he was a hard man to pin down but maybe he didn't pass the psychological tests to make it in, which was probably a blessing.

It wasn't really something I had ever considered. Loads of offers had come my way and I never really fancied it. The experience in there was a bit of a laugh at the time, but, looking back on it, I can hardly believe some of the stuff that went on. The actor Stephen Baldwin was on another planet!

As it happened, the fee came in very handy for a totally unexpected tax bill of £350,000. It was never made public, but it was threatening to erupt all the way through the time I was appearing on the show. Good old HMRC, picking up on the mess of some old companies I had set up years before and, in all honesty, had forgotten about.

They were getting so heavy and keen to make an example of a big name that at one point they were preparing to literally march into the Big Brother house and present me with the bill!

I have always trusted whoever is looking after me to sort all of that stuff out on my behalf. It wasn't a personal tax bill: it was company tax. My accountant Steven Ross dealt with it all. He described it as 'mayhem' when I was happily dossing around with the American TV personality and former madam Heidi Fleiss and Stephen Baldwin!

I came out of the house, which was like *One Flew Over the Cuckoo's Nest*, and the next day went straight to HMRC and wrote them a cheque.

I sat down and asked if they wanted to do a deal. They said no deals. I said, 'OK, I'm an honourable British bloke flying the flag for this country abroad, my son is a serving soldier and there is no way in the world I will be accused of ducking my responsibility as a taxpayer. If that's what I owe, tell me how much I am due.'

I simply wasn't aware of it, so I took it on the chin. I am not a Starbucks or a Google; I'm not hiding in America or running anywhere.

They were like wolves foaming at the mouth waiting to sink their teeth in. They thought there was going to be a big screaming match, a bit of pantomime with me going nuts. I felt insulted, in all honesty.

Alex Cole first came on the scene when Pete introduced me to him in 2006 and he really has been great for us. It was the arm I didn't have round me any more because I was in LA so much, and Alex stepped in and said, 'This is how it's going to be.' He basically runs our lives for us.

I'm now godfather to his little girl Sienna. I've got very close to them. He's not just my manager: I'm also his best mate and he's been fantastic for us in Los Angeles. We're producing content together, we've got great offices in LA, we've got lads writing for us and we're progressing with our business.

He is still looking after other talent but I really feel like I'm growing up and getting more businesswise, now that we work together. When I was in football everyone said, 'Look after your money.' But, when you're young and you've only got your cock to keep, you don't think of any of that.

Pete helped that transition to being a film star. I like being in the trenches with the boys, with a strong leader above me to direct my actions, and Pete was that man for over a decade. When he said it would make more sense for me to work with Alex, I fell into line and agreed immediately. Alex is a British guy and knows LA inside out, with loads of contacts, so it made sense.

Pete started looking after Marco Pierre White and that was a real issue for me. It rubbed me up the wrong way. When my mate, the restaurateur Tony Allen, flew out for *Snatch* in LA, he had just written a cheque to Marco Pierre White for over a million in a libel case. I didn't agree with it. I thought they should have sorted it out between them rather than go through the courts. I thought it was wrong that Marco took that money from Tony. It wasn't just Tony he took it from: it was from his kids too, effectively, and there was no need for that in my opinion.

Pete had a birthday party at his pizza place in Chelsea in 2012 and that was our last real night out. He knew how strongly I felt about the situation. Pete introduced me to Marco. He put his hand out and I said, 'I ain't shaking your hand.' It was very, very awkward. I stuck to my principles. I just couldn't shake his hand with all that had gone on.

That was sort of a wedge between me and Pete in a lot of ways. Nothing was said about it until I next came back from LA. Pete was insisting he pick me up. He was starting up a bookmaker's, which we all invested in, and he said, 'I'm going to go into this business and run it. You've got Alex now and I don't think you need anyone in England.'

It was a big shock to me.

It was a huge loss because Pete and I were joined at the hip for a long time. It really knocked me for six hearing those words tumble out. We had a few tears over it afterwards.

I said, 'Pete, ten or eleven years, everything we've been through and you tell me this pulling off the M25!'

I was shell-shocked. When you're so close to someone for such a long time it's like a very close relative passing away. The bookmaker's business didn't work out and I lost my investment, but he gave it his best shot. He always did.

Time has moved on and I'm doing my thing and he's opened a restaurant in London. I love him dearly, but we're not on the phone every week or every month. Pete's still a brother. If I ever needed something really badly, I would phone him.

You move on in life. I've found after finishing football how much you move on from people, especially with me – I'm all or nothing.

This is my team, these are my boys in the dressing room. I had it growing up with the Bedmond boys. You never thought it was going to break up, then one of the boys gets a girlfriend and stops coming out, then they start falling like dominoes.

If I saw any one of the lads I played with it would be a hug and a cuddle straight away.

That recurs in my life, it's happened with the movies, but I think I've got tougher with it and accepted it, and I can deal with it better.

The number-one person who is there when you turn round is your wife. It has always been Tanya. The ups and downs with money, air rage, the Sioux Falls fight, the nose biting – we've been through everything and you turn around and this angel is still there.

Tanya had been there for me through thick and thin, but I was about to risk everything that mattered to me over a stupid night out in Russia on a show I was so proud to be producing for National Geographic.

That dog is always poking his angry head out of the kennel, and my marriage to Tanya was to face its biggest test in twenty years as a result.

20

Russian Roulette

It was a proud moment for me when I started working with National Geographic. I was doing something for the first time where I was starring in a documentary and also producing it. When we were doing the original planning for the series, it was shaping up to be a hell of a trip.

They wanted me to initially commit to two months of filming in Russia, which was a big ask to be away from Tans for that amount of time. We decided that the best way for it to work would be for me to go to Russia for a month, then come back to London to meet up with her for two weeks and then go back and finish the final month of filming.

We got out there late in 2012 and it really was something special. I spent time working on their huge rail network, then as a bodyguard in Moscow with full close-protection training. I then worked on a massive industrial project, in some terrifying manual labour where some guys had lost their lives. I also worked in the great outdoors and came dangerously close to death again when we found ourselves in the worst possible position with a grizzly bear – between her food and her cubs. I worked in arduous conditions and really mucked in – there were no shortcuts and I think the end result was worth the effort. *Russia's Toughest* is a series I am really proud of. We were all over Russia in tanks and helicopters, living in tents, really getting into it and experiencing life in the wild. It was a dream for me given my history with the outdoors – only this time it was a step up, with grizzly bears and fishing for leaping salmon.

After a few weeks of solid filming deep in the countryside, we had to go back to Moscow. We stayed at the Radisson for three or four days. We were going out in the mornings and filming a bit of bodyguarding stuff. I was training up to be a fully qualified close-protection officer and had to go through the formal training courses.

In the evenings, we were going out and practising what we had learned in the day for real. We were looking after 'Mrs Russia', Alisa Krylova. It was mind-boggling to see the wealth on show. She would be driving around town in a Ferrari and the bodyguards would be close behind in a Bentley. It was big time. We were out working and all was going well, and we had gone back one night to watch a football match in the main bar at the hotel.

The interpreter came in with another lad and a girl, who they said was a singer and actress. She had a fake tattoo on her forehead and was decked out in furs. She came over and we were introduced. We had a chat, she asked for a picture and of course I agreed.

Later on during our stay in Moscow, we found ourselves filming more bodyguarding stuff at a Mercedes event, and the same Russian girl was there again. We were working with the two bodyguards of Alisa's and the film crew. This girl was hovering around, again with the interpreter and this other fella, and she asked for another picture. I thought nothing of it and said yes again, then off we went. That was it, end of the night – job done.

We did some more stuff with Alisa around the shops the next day and that was our lot. Moscow filming done. We knocked off at about 8 p.m. and the film crew decided to go to a bar close to the hotel. It was a really good craic and was probably the first time we had really let our hair down properly during the shoot.

But then the Russian girl, the fella and the interpreter showed up – again. We all said hello. She was on the other side of the table and we didn't really speak all that much. The interpreter then started saying his friend wanted to throw a wrap party for the boys. He was saying we had worked hard, and I must admit the interpreter, Olivier, was an impressive lad – French but he spoke loads of languages.

So anyway all the lads decided it would be a good idea to go back to this bloke's apartment. I was a split second away from not going and just calling it a night – but then that big bastard dog of mine emerged from the kennel.

In the end, I decided to go for a bit. We were meant to be going home two days later so I thought, Why not?

We got dropped off at this incredible apartment and there were loads of people there, drinking and having a good laugh. People on the balcony, in the living room, milling around.

There was another guy at the party called André, a multi-millionaire who I had acted as a bodyguard for as part of the documentary. He had a Mercedes Maybach and was proper big-time. Over there, if you've got money, you're a big star.

He came up to me and said he wanted to take me for dinner after the party. I said I couldn't leave the lads. Then an hour, two, three, four went past.

The Russian girl turned up. There was a photo here and a photo there. Every time I turned around to talk to someone, she was hovering.

I should have known something was up – but that big bastard dog just wanted me to carry on drinking.

I should have just said there and then, 'That's me done – I'm out of here.' But I didn't.

Finally, at about 2 a.m., I decided to call it a night – and the girl and these two fellas were there. They said they were going back home and could give us a lift to the hotel. We got out onto the street outside this grand main entrance and one of the blokes called a car over and told the driver to take us back to the Radisson.

I admit now that I'd had way too much to drink, but the next thing I know I've been spun round and was being kissed by this Russian girl.

We then get back to London a day or so later and I go off to meet Tans. We had booked Shendish Manor, a hotel near Hemel, and I got back there to see her. All the family were there, everything was great and we were having a really good time.

Next thing, my manager Alex phoned me. He said, 'What happened the other night in Russia with the blonde bird?'

I said, 'What you on about?'

He said: 'My mum's sister, my aunt, lives in Moscow and their equivalent of TMZ [a showbiz website in the States] have a video of you snogging a bird in the street.'

Before he could even finish, my heart was in my stomach. I felt sick.

I was thirty yards away from my family, my wife and all my friends in the bar at the hotel. I'd had a few drinks before this point and was a little bit drunk.

So I just buried my head in the sand and tried to ignore it.

I said to Alex, 'I've got to sort this out and I've got to sort myself out.'

He is very close to Tans and he said, 'You've got to tell her.'

I told him, 'I will sort this out. I will put it right – this is the last straw for me.'

I had completely let myself down. I had let everybody down.

The next day, the reality really dawned on me. I got through the previous day because the bravery liquid was in me and I thought I could deal with it. But I couldn't. For every minute that passed, it was going through my head and it was eating me up.

I was due to go back to Russia to film the second part of the series for a month and Tans was heading back to LA the following day.

We had woken up at the hotel, had had a bit of room service and were having a cup of tea in the room. Then the phone rang. Tans answered it.

I just heard her say, 'What? Who? What do you want?'

It was a reporter from a tabloid newspaper and I could see the life drain out of her. She gave the phone to me and the bloke said he was from a paper and told me, 'Vinnie. We've got a video of you kissing a Russian girl.'

In one way I was relieved it was out because I couldn't carry it around with me. It was an awful, awful thing. A sickening thing. So now I could face it and I told him how it was. It was a stitch-up.

Alex sent me the Web link of the story and I looked at it. I have only ever seen the video once because I am so embarrassed, disgusted and gutted about it. It is just unwatchable.

When you see it, you can see they were set up with a camera on the roof above us and she basically got to her mark and made her move. It was the only point they could film me around there and get a clear shot. You can hear them talking on the video and sussing out whether it is definitely me.

So at this point I was just totally relieved I had to deal with it and just get my cards on the table. I have always been the kind of person who can't hold anything in. It kills you when you have got something like that on your conscience. You just have to put your hands up and deal with it.

Tans was sitting there in front of me and she was going nuts. I put the phone down and she went fucking ballistic. I had nothing to say to her other than repeating, 'I'm sorry, I'm sorry, I'm sorry.'

She phoned her mum, who came and picked her up. I was in no-man's-land. I was absolutely shell-shocked and didn't know what to do.

I spoke to a friend of mine at the *Sun* because we just needed to get our side of the story out as quickly as possible. Any little bit of publicity this girl could get, she was going for it.

I was reading on the Internet that I had supposedly been seeing her for a year! This was total rubbish.

I am not screaming and shouting about her. I have to make that clear. I walked into this. It is something I have to take on the chin.

I stayed at Shendish Manor all day. I couldn't eat and was totally lost. My sister Ann came up later on and, if memory serves me correctly, called me 'a stupid bastard'.

But she couldn't just leave me there sitting on my own. Ann stayed with me that night and I had to go back to Russia – the worst scenario on the planet. Going back there and not getting to see Tans.

She wouldn't answer the phone to me. I had to finish the job, though – there was a whole crew out there waiting for me to get back to start filming again.

Tans then headed back to Los Angeles and there was a media circus waiting for her. It just breaks my heart that she had to go through that because of me.

I was contracted to National Geographic, so I went back to Russia, but I was in bits. I couldn't wait to get the job done and go home. It was the longest month of my life. There were twenty years together on the line: we'd been married nineteen and were together for two years as a couple before that.

You never know for sure what the outcome is going to be when you are in the middle of something like that, but that is definitely the lowest I have seen her in all the time we have been together.

We have got a lot of work still to do but we both love each other more than anything on the planet and that is getting us through. That is why, for the first time in my life, I have started seeing a psychologist. I needed to finally put an end to this carnage I seem to cause every now and again.

Whether it was Sioux Falls and having the massive fight that nearly blinded me, or when I was arrested for fighting with the neighbour we fell out with in Hertfordshire or biting the reporter's nose in Ireland, I've always been involved in something that has upset the apple cart. I want to live a peaceful life now without any drama. The way I hoped to achieve that was by spending time with the psychologist and talking with him.

I needed to listen to his views and get to the root of it. What was it that led me into these situations? Was it the breakup of my parents' marriage when I was a boy? Was it leaving home when I was sixteen with all my worldly belongings in a couple of black bin liners? Was it living on my mates' sofas for years, a different one every night? Was it working at the college kitchens in Bradfield when I was a teenager? That was fucking horrendous.

There is a lot of psychological stuff that has gone on. Living with John and Wendy Moore, my old football manager and his wife, was the first security I felt I had before I moved into a house with my mate Robbo in Hemel.

I didn't speak to my old man for three years – I would ring Ann secretly from a payphone but hang up if he or my stepmum Jenny answered.

A lot of damage had been done; it was time to do something about it. Maybe I should have gone to see someone years ago.

I feel great in myself right now. It has helped a lot. That big bastard dog is well and truly in the kennel right now and that's where I plan to keep it for the rest of my days.

The National Geographic show airs at the end of 2013 and everyone will see the graft that went into it.

21

Spud and Kaley

It was heartbreaking seeing the pain on Tanya's face, and answering to Aaron and Kaley was even harder to take.

The first thing I do in a situation when I'm in the wrong is shut everyone out. The shame of what I've done makes me react like that. I've closed myself off when I've messed up before. Whether it was biting that reporter Ted Oliver in Ireland or nearly getting blinded in the bar fight in Sioux Falls, that's how I've reacted.

I then realise I have to take care of my immediate family.

You end up talking about how you can deal with it, how you can sort it all out and get your life back on track. You go through all the heartache and the explanations – how it could have happened, what you can learn from it. And you hope you can move on and that it brings everyone closer.

You look at people who have gone through similar things and I think it makes you stronger as a family. I think it brings you closer. You have to learn from it, and ask, 'How can we make sure this doesn't happen again?'

I look back and it shocks me how much pain one person's actions can cause. When I've got myself in scrapes, and then there are the headlines, I look at Tans's face and think, If I hadn't done that, I wouldn't have caused all this hurt. Seeing the grief on my wife's face has been punishment enough every time things go off track.

But then I sit down with my family and some things put it all into perspective. You think about things like the heartbreaking case of Madeleine McCann, the little girl who was abducted in Portugal a few days before her fourth birthday, and it makes you think that you can get through your problems.

After it all blew over, Tans and I were back to sitting up in the cabana every night. We talk about how well we've done, how lucky we are, how hard we work, what great friends we have and how we've built a beautiful home together. Tans is there for me, looks after me, and is there for Kaley, too. We have one of Kaley's friends, Chloe Bale, living with us while she tries to make it as an actress, so Tans is like a mother to them both. And then there are the dogs and the constant stream of visitors from home to attend to.

It took Tans and me until 16 June 2010 to get our green cards and become permanent residents of the USA. It took years to sort out and the only way to do it was officially and with all the right people being employed to see it through, which was worth every penny.

But it helps no end that we moved to America, away from the home in Hertfordshire. That was where I had trouble with the neighbour, and it's where I wandered into the woods with the intention of shooting myself. We'd had some beautiful times there, but it held too many memories that needed to be left behind.

It petrified me that the new life we'd created away from all that could have slipped away because I'd let my guard down and the dog out. I'm doing my best to make sure it stays up.

The one area of my life where I can hold my head high is that I've never messed with drugs – no matter how many times I've been offered the stuff. My nose is witness to that. There's not a soul on this planet who could say they've ever seen me take cocaine.

I've seen so many people destroyed by the gear. And I've seen what I'm like on the drink. I always think that, if I started to do drugs, the wheels would fall off completely. It's not for me.

My wife has to take drugs every day to stay alive. So, if I ever caught anybody doing them for a laugh in my house, I'm sure I'd be unstoppable. My actions would be unbearable. To my knowledge, no one has done drugs while they've been at my place. They say everyone's at it these days, taking them recreationally on a Friday night or whatever. I just don't want them near me or my family. I've walked into a toilet and been offered drugs. A year ago I went in and there were three guys there doing it, and they were like, 'Oh, Vin, we're not sure if there's enough to go around.' I was like, 'Fuck, you boys carry on.' I had a piss and that was that. If you want to do that, go ahead. Just don't do it at my house.

I've never touched marijuana, either. I smoked cigars right through playing football, but I've been off even those for the five years up to the time of writing. After about three years I joined a golf club and the lad I played with most days was an Armenian who was a proper chain smoker. One day I had a cigarette with him and then got into them. Before I went home I'd get the mouthwash and chewing gum going to hide the smell from Tanya. Then one day Wally spilled the beans about the mouthwash and gum, and Tans said to me, 'You bugger.' It's like everything: start off with one or two and then it goes from there and gets out of hand. I try to limit them as much as I can.

I'm trying to stay fit – for my career and my family. Keeping healthy gets me thinking about the future these days. Everyone wants to be around to see their kids get married and have families of their own. As I am writing this book, I have gone nearly six months without a single drink.

Smoking is obviously no good for anybody, but, if that's the only bad vice I've got, I reckon I'm doing OK. I'm conscious of it, though, and every night I go to bed saying I'm going to give up the smokes tomorrow. Then you get on a film set and there's all the boredom between takes, so you have a cigarette to fill the time and all of a sudden you're chain smoking.

Being married to a girl who is half Irish doesn't help, either. I love coming home to my favourite meals – shepherd's pie and Irish stew, with fry-ups for breakfast. I'd say bread is my downfall, so I have to watch all that type of food. The roles I play require me to stay in shape and I love it when people say, 'You've dropped a bit of weight – you look well.' So that's a big motivation.

But that's only part of it. The need to stay healthy goes back to the panic attacks about dying that I had when I was a seven-year-old kid. I haven't had those same petrifying feelings recently, or thought about dying as much.

But, when I say I'll be fifty in 2015, that does scare me. Luckily I don't feel like I'm nearing fifty. My dad's seventy and he's fit as a fiddle. I'd love to be like that.

Nan wasn't as lucky. When she couldn't live at home any more she was moved to a care home, at the age of 93. My Aunt Margaret was round the corner and was very good to her. It was heart-wrenching for me because she went in after I moved to America, and she'd always said to me, 'Look after me when I'm old.' I always grew up thinking she would never end up in a home because she'd made that plea.

I changed my mind when I saw that she needed care only a home could provide. I saw her suffer the Benjamin Button syndrome: it was like watching her slowly regress back to the state of a baby, where she was helpless and couldn't do a thing for herself.

The last time I saw her she'd started to refuse to come out of her room. She didn't know who anyone was any more, but still recognised my voice. She'd get all teary and very emotional, and the only thing I could do was sit there and say, 'Yeah, it's me, Nan, it's me.'

We eventually took her out of the room and put her back at around three o'clock in the afternoon. Tans and I tucked her in and she said to me, 'Come here and give me a kiss.' I gave her a little peck and she said, 'I'll always love you.' She pulled the covers over herself and snuggled up. I caught a plane back to America the next day and she died when I was in the air.

It was absolutely heartbreaking and it took me a long time to get over the thought that I was travelling when she passed away. That was 2012.

Now all I'm thinking about is the future, and what my kids will be doing.

It would be great to have a grandson or granddaughter. I know this family would be great with them. My dad, mum, stepmum and stepdad are all still alive. My sister Ann is still roaring around Watford like a single version of me, and Tanya's mum, dad and brother are all still here. That's a great family and they'd love to see grandkids as part of it.

Kaley calls me Vin, which I love. I've never had a problem with that.

All this talk of grandkids and marriage is down the line, though. For now, I just want Spud back safe from his time in the army.

When he went into the army, that was it – he was a man and it was up to him. He's a massive royalist. That's why he went in. Aaron could sit down and write his own book about the monarchy and British history. It's his big interest and it's all self-taught. It's like me with shooting, fishing and wildlife: he loves Britain, the army, Winston Churchill and history just as much. By the time he was seventeen he could talk to any army officer far older than he was and teach them something – it's in his blood. He's very, very patriotic and he'd defend the country on his own, the little bugger.

I got choked up when I watched Aaron pass out of army training college. He was seventeen, which brings me back to another one of those little coincidences. I was seventeen when my old pal

Cal and I went to try to join up to fight in the Falklands. I'm not sure why we were refused but maybe we were too young.

Another parallel between me and Aaron is that we both lost our driving licences at nineteen. And he got exactly the same ban as I did. He was staying with me and Tans at the Grove Hotel near Watford a couple of years into his service and we had a drink. He was on duty early the next morning so had to jump in the car at half past five in the morning to get back to his barracks on time. A copper spotted him running a traffic light and pulled him over, even though there was no one else on the road.

The cop also breathalysed him and it turned out he was just over the limit. He told this cop he was a soldier on his way back to barracks, but he nicked him anyway. I couldn't believe it. He was nearly there, not even a mile from the barracks on his way to serve his country, and that copper did him anyway. Spud is not the kind of lad who would just get in a car steaming drunk. There is remorse. He got an eighteen-month ban in court. I just said to him, 'It's going to cut your legs from under you now, mate, but you'll get through it.' There would be no good in screaming and shouting at him because the only person who deserved a bollocking was that cop.

Aaron's getting slapped with a driving ban has been the least of my worries when it comes to him over the past six years. He's in the Household Cavalry, because it's one of the oldest divisions in the British Army and he loves all the pomp and circumstance that goes with it.

I thank God he hasn't served in Afghanistan yet. He came close in 2011, when his regiment were told to prepare to ship out for a tour of duty, but it got called off. I think of that as getting lucky. I've been to a hospital to see injured soldiers and it's soul-destroying for me to think Aaron could end up there. Aaron's serving in Afghanistan is something I've put at the back of my mind and refused to think about until he's on the plane.

I think it would be nice after six years if he says, 'I've done my bit,' and comes home. If he was sitting with me now I'd say, 'Son, I think you've served your time.'

He's going to have to make a decision about his future when his six years are up. If he doesn't want to stay on, there is always a place for him at home with me. Tans would love to have him with us, and I want to have Aaron and Kaley at close quarters.

I want to see Aaron come home and maybe work towards getting his pilot's licence. He loves flying and has been doing it from a young age. One of the most fantastic things to happen to me in my life was having helicopter lessons at Elstree. When I saw Aaron up there too in a plane it was amazing. He started at about fourteen, and he'll be twenty-two by the time this book comes out, and his getting his pilot's licence is what I would like to see happen by then.

I've got a lot to be proud of with my kids. I'll never forget the day I got an email from a friend of mine at a tabloid paper. It was from the premiere of the first James Bond film starring Daniel Craig. The journalist Gordon Smart, who helped me write this book, needed to get a soldier for a picture with Daniel Craig – it was the only way Daniel would pose up for the *Sun*. Sweaty, as I call him because he's a Sweaty Sock or 'Jock', grabbed the first bloke in uniform he could find.

It turns out it was Aaron and they ended up having a night on the tiles at the after party. That is some picture – Spud and James Bond!

Sadly, 007 and the licence to kill is one film role that has escaped me now. But, then again, I've got a blockbuster on the way with the biggest names in the action movie business.

22

Sly and the Family Jones

After fifteen years I actually feel as if my career is brewing up to take off again.

I did say after *X-Men 3* I'd never go in and do prosthetics again with brutal four-hour sessions in the chair – but then NBC offered me a big role, to play a character called Scales in the TV series *The Cape* in 2010.

The series was filmed at Gower Studios, two miles from my house, so it was ideal. I could get on a pushbike and free-wheel down the hill and I'd be there in ten minutes. I'm not so sure about cycling back up the hill, though: the lungs might not have it in them any more.

We were commissioned for twelve shows. Then at work one day, while we were filming the tenth episode, some executives came down from NBC and said, 'These are the last scenes we're doing today.' You can be as positive as you like about Hollywood, but it's a precarious game.

Around the same time I was in a big show for NBC called *Chuck* as a guest star. It's a spy comedy and quite a big deal out in the US, so it paved the way for some other good roles.

Things started looking up when I got a big part in *Elementary* with Jonny Lee Miller, the Sherlock Holmes series. It's a quality show and has been a huge ratings hit out here and back home. I got some rave reviews for it in America. I probably got more recognition for that than the last ten movies I've done! TV out here is the way to be noticed and helps you land more parts. I was ticking along for a few years and then *Elementary* happened, and all of a sudden the phones don't stop ringing.

Psych is another show I'm on right now as I write this. It's in its eighth season and a guest-star slot has now landed me a part as a main character. It's a great honour.

Scandal aside, the Nat Geo documentary, which comes out at the end of 2013, is something I am fiercely proud of. Film scripts are still pouring in and, if it all goes wrong, I've got an open door into football punditry in the US, covering all the Premier League games. Let's face it, if Piers Morgan is doing it, I think I might have a bit more to offer!

I have been lucky – bagging some big parts I've told you about in the book along the way, from *Snatch* and *Swordfish* through to *X-Men 3* and *Hell Ride*. But the biggest is due out in 2013, with Sylvester Stallone and Arnold Schwarzenegger in *Escape Plan*.

Sly Stallone is probably one of the biggest icons I've ever met. The *Rocky* movies had such a big influence on me. I was just overwhelmed with the action, the acting and the emotion on the screen. Those movies were a huge motivation for us all as players, too. I watched them over and over again as the triumph over adversity and never-say-die attitude came through. Again, it made working with Sylvester Stallone all the more special after the years watching the films first time around.

I first met Sly in the least glamorous surroundings you could imagine. I got a call to go out to his offices in South Beverly Hills in 2010 because he wanted me to be a character in *Rambo IV*. As you can imagine, I was very nervous about this one and wanted to make a good impression.

His office was only a couple of blocks from the famous Rodeo Drive in Beverly Hills, but it was a funny-looking place. You'd never think that one of the biggest stars in the world would have his HQ in this bland, beige building.

There was a big fella at the bottom of the steps and all Pete Burrell and I could see was a stairway leading into the building. I cleared my throat and said to the bloke, 'We're here to see Mr Stallone.' It was making me chuckle even as I was saying it.

So the big lump gets on the radio. I'm still on the pavement outside with Pete at the time, and he suddenly says, 'Head up there, gentlemen.'

I always remember the cigar smoke smell. Pete was a massive wine and cigar connoisseur and had done all his homework in preparation. He knew Sly loved a cigar, so Pete brought him the best cigar he could get his hands on. I remember him turning round to me on the way up saying, 'If this doesn't get us the part, nothing will.'

I was a bit nervous about Pete kissing his arse. I always try to play situations like that really cool and not make a fuss.

So we take a seat in his office and the next thing he comes walking in. All of a sudden, here he was, in the flesh, my idol from the *Rocky* and *Rambo* movies – you just can't take it in.

We did all the handshakes and then he said, 'I want to show you something. We've just got the trailer in about half an hour ago. What do you think?'

What did I think? Even if it was crap I'd say it was brilliant, the best thing I had seen, and suddenly I was kissing his arse!

Once we got all that out the way, we cracked on with business. He was impressive like that, changed gear in the meeting really well. He said, 'I've told the producers I don't want to even see anyone else. This is your part.'

I was absolutely delighted to hear one of my screen heroes saying that. I cherished every second of it. We left and the next thing I heard, I was booking time in the diary to shoot in Australia. It was a bit of a pain because they didn't give us any idea of time – whether it was two, three or four months on the other side of the world.

During all of the diary haggling with Sly's people, another film came up – *Midnight Meat Train* with Bradley Cooper. It was due to be filming around the same time as *Rambo* – but in LA, which was really handy for me.

I couldn't get a straight answer from the *Rambo* about when the movie was going to happen and the other movie started to play hardball, threatening to recast the part I was offered if I hung on any longer.

With a heavy heart, I sent the bad news back to Sly's producers saying I had to commit elsewhere. It was a sickener, but something I had to do.

A few years went by and I got friendly with Sly's brother, Frank Stallone. He said, 'You should have just called the office and told them what happened and Sylvester would have kicked those producers' asses. You were his number-one choice! The other fella they got in, he wasn't Sylvester's choice.'

All was not lost.

Next thing we got a call for an audition for a movie called *The Tomb*, which has been renamed *Escape Plan* now. The same producer came on to me and said, 'We want you in this movie.'

It comes out in October 2013. It's a great action movie. I got on with Sly really well. He was giving me golf lessons in the studio! We were on this huge stage preparing for a massive fight scene, which took about three days to film. Between takes, he was showing me all these golf swings – he nearly took the assistant director's head off showing me how to turn the wrists! He went and got his assistant to get his driver out the car – he was a real man's man.

I have a picture I am really proud of, with three directors' chairs lined up together. One with 'Sylvester Stallone', another with 'Arnold Schwarzenegger' and the third, tucked neatly in the middle, reads, 'Vinnie Jones'. It was another moment in my life where I had to pinch myself. I was so, so proud to be making a movie with the biggest names in the business.

It was strange to start with, on set. I was always worried in the early days turning up without much direction about what I should look like. There was no mention of being clean-shaven, or whether I should have my head shaved, or wear my hair a bit longer. I turned up on this film with a massive budget and some-one looks at me and goes, 'Yeah, that's fine.'

The first time I saw the director of what is a $70 million movie – a hundred million dollars by the time it's on the screen – he asked if I've played any golf! No mention of the actual job.

I had a few scenes with Arnie. Within a few minutes of meet-ing him we got talking about soccer. He knew that I played for Chelsea and I had a bit of a reputation back in the day. That's normally how my conversations start with actors of that stature. It doesn't matter if it's Sly or Arnie, they're all fascinated that I played at such a high level of football because sport is such a mas-sive thing there. Arnie especially has a real respect for it, because he was at the top of his game as a bodybuilder and understands the sacrifices you have to make and dedication you have to give to get anywhere.

We shot the film down in New Orleans, so I got sorted out with a golf membership down there and it flew by. I enjoyed working with them and I'd love to do something with them again in the future – I'd be mad not to.

Weirdly enough, Sly's business partner and right-hand man is a guy called Kevin from Liverpool. He started out at the bottom with Sly and now they are partners. I keep in contact with Sly through him. Perhaps that goal at Anfield for Chelsea back in the day wasn't the best move for my career after all. At the end of the movie I gave Sly a pair of brown George Cleverly brogues, as I'm friends with the Glasgow family – he loved them. I hope he also had some more made by the boys.

The next big movie I am working on is the story of Wales rugby legend Gareth Thomas, who came out as gay in 2009. One of my best mates in Hollywood is Mickey Rourke, and he's playing Thomas.

We're getting the finance in place for the film, so we'll probably start filming in October or November. It's a great story and Mickey is a tremendous actor, as well as a tremendous bloke. I play his mentor in the film, the bloke he comes out to in Soho when he is at the peak of his fame – and a married man. I've already made it absolutely clear, though – I said to Mickey, 'I ain't kissing your white arse!'

He loves coming up to the house. I may be in a restaurant and he'll ring up. He's on speed dial and we chat about four times a week. He asks what we are up to and the next thing he is inviting us over to his house where he is having a tattoo by a guy called Mark Mahoney, a celebrity tattoo artist. I was there getting one done and this young pop singer came in before she was famous – Rihanna. She's made a bit of a name for herself!

Anyway, I've got Wally Downes with me and we are in Mickey's house watching him get a tattoo. The next thing Wally has got his shirt off and is getting a tattoo done by Mickey!

We all headed back to our house and I've got this great picture of me, Rhino, Jay Statham and Mickey playing darts.

He blends in with the Hollywood All Stars lads – no problem at all. It's as if he were part of the team.

Tanya always says to me, 'You don't have to feel that you owe everybody.' I just feel that I'm very lucky to be where I am and how my life's turned out. I hate to see people struggle and I'll always do my best to help out and be as generous as I can afford to be.

When I played I was a good leader of men. With the All Stars boys, I will ring Tans up and get her to buy twenty steaks in and get the barbecue on the go. All the lads come up with their kids and we get them all playing by the pool.

LA has given me some beautiful memories and football is still a huge part of that. When we first got here with Hollywood United we would have some young lads in their teens kicking about. All those boys are now parents and I can see a new generation coming through.

The whole magic of football out here was being in Beverly Hills, jumping through a hole in the fence and putting two jumpers down. It was no different from the spirit at Woodlands back in the day, except that the people have more dosh. Harry Bassett has been replaced by people like Robbie Williams, Steve Jones and Rod Stewart and all sorts of other characters.

I've got some great pictures of me and the now retired cricketer Freddie Flintoff from a couple of years ago when we won the trophy and he came to watch with his kids. Kelsey Grammer has been up to watch and then gone for a night out with the boys after. Ruud Gullit has played; so have Richard Gough and Mario Melchiot; Robbie Keane has come along from LA Galaxy to watch, too. I played against him when he was a kid coming through at Wolves. He played against me on his debut; he said he was shitting himself.

He said I was chasing after him shouting, 'I'm going to rip your arse out, boy!' He's a funny lad. We've been asked to leave the Beverly Hills Hotel for being too raucous over the last year or so. He's a great new addition to the crowd of expats out here.

Celeb-wise Mark Wright has turned out recently and Ricky Whittle, while he is over here trying to make it as an actor.

For all the famous faces and the Hollywood lifestyle, it's funny how it all comes back to football.

Reading this book, you would think the FA Cup medal would be my most treasured possession, but the relationships, friendships and memories are actually worth a lot more to me than a little bit of metal.

I gave my FA Cup winner's medal to Aaron when he was sort of old enough to recognise its importance. He loved it and his mates used to love looking at it. After a few years it was misplaced, but I needed it for a photoshoot. I eventually dug it out at the bottom of one of his toy boxes.

I kept it at home for a while in LA, and it was nice, because I've got a lovely trophy cabinet with all the acting and football medals, and people used to like seeing it. But AFC Wimbledon were calling and I'm all for them. I thought it was time to give the medal back to them, really. When MK Dons handed back all the silverware and memorabilia, that was it for me. They had no link with the Wimbledon I knew and loved. AFC Wimbledon is the heart of that club now. I think if you mention Wimbledon my name is the first to come up. I'm probably more connected to it now than Dave Bassett or Joe Kinnear. So now the medal sits proudly in the AFC Wimbledon trophy cabinet, hopefully for many years to come.

In January 2012 I was given a commemorative marble stone at Wembley for my services to the FA cup. It is placed not far from the Bobby Moore statue and it's something I'm really proud of. I had another one made, which is now part of the paving next to our swimming pool in LA.

I was almost going to give it to auction to raise money for

Princess Diana's memorial in London, but my dad stopped me. She presented it to me and I felt strongly about doing that. I'm glad I didn't in the end, because I think it's in the right place now. I'll probably give the Leeds United medal I got when we won the Second Division league back to Leeds for their trophy cabinet, too.

With Tanya's heart condition all these things pale into insignificance – Sly, Arnie, celebrity and football. And that's why I took on a job that I am more proud of than anything – and now find myself recognised more for than giving Steve McMahon something to think about in 1988.

23

The Bedmond Bee Gee

As I write this, it has been twenty-six years since Tans had open-heart surgery. Her heart collapsed during childbirth so, when it comes round to Kaley's birthday, she still becomes fragile – even though she has become better at coping with it as the years have gone by. Kaley's birthday is a reminder, on 15 April: we realise it's been another year (she actually had her operation on 20 May).

I could not imagine being without Tans. She's great – terrific personality, beautiful and when she's on form she lights up a room. It is my job to be positive and be strong and pick her up when she gets down. That's how we get through the day. She looks after the house, dogs, Kaley and me – it's a day-to-day thing. She will get scared, and I will listen to her heart and see if it is regular. I will reassure her and deal with it like that, but there is no cloud over our house.

We first got together when we were twelve; then our first kiss was at sixteen. I was never going to get married, not in a million years. I certainly wasn't top of her dad's list, either! If you properly fall in love, that's all it is. Some people are meant to be married in this life.

She puts up with me and her Irish roots help with that. She forgives my late nights and my insistence on having everyone round the house whenever I can persuade them to join us. I've put her through the mill a few times – when that bloody dog gets the better of me – but she knows I would move heaven and earth for her, Kaley and Aaron.

The trauma she went through in surgery has meant we have never been able to have children, but I have a beautiful boy, she has a beautiful girl and we both regard them as our own. The day I officially adopted Kaley meant so much to me. I'm proud we've been able to bring them up as our own and give them a good life.

The worst part for Tanya in the early years after the transplant was her annual checkup, the angiogram. She still needs to have it today. I have been there for every one – sitting there waiting patiently and nervously outside. It is a major examination and, even though she is drugged up, she is conscious the whole time. She's made me promise I'll be waiting there after every one. The promise isn't necessary. I wouldn't be anywhere else. Sometimes she would come out crying and I'd just think, This isn't fair, this isn't fair. It's an immediate reaction to Tanya's discomfort, not a complaint.

Tanya clings to me after these checkups and I say to her, 'I'll always be here for you.'

Where we are in our lives now is new territory. They simply haven't got any research about what happens twenty-odd years after an operation like that. It's like smoking: everybody was doing it for years and years then someone worked out that it was bad for your health. We are going through the same thing with the medication she is taking to stop her body rejecting a vital organ.

The drugs she has to take to keep her heart on track are heavy-duty and they are now beginning to have a knock-on effect, so every day we are on our guard and extra-vigilant. One of the things we have to deal with is the danger of skin cancer as a side effect, so we have to keep a very close eye on that. She loves the sunshine and the warm weather in LA but she has to be more careful than ever. She recently had some skin taken away and she's got a scar where it was cut out. She's got little scars all over her as a result of similar procedures. They are reminders about what we need to do every day.

We are lucky that the doctors we see are the best in the business. She's got a brilliant skin doctor she goes to and, after a lot of time and effort, she has now found a quality heart doctor here, too. We fly back to the UK regularly and keep in touch with the staff at Harefield Hospital, who know her medical history. She's got one lump on her lip that has caused some concern. They have to cut a bit out, then test it and, if they find any malignant tumours, they will have to get right in there and cut it out. We have no other option but to just keep soldiering on.

We have worked out our own way to deal with it. We just put it at the back of our minds. It's not something we make a big deal out of and not something we talk about a lot. We try to live an absolutely normal life.

You see all these amputees returning from Afghanistan, brave guys, saying their injuries won't affect them. You have to get on with it and that's what Tans has done and we have done as a family over the years. If we find a lump or a bump, we have to deal with it and that's that.

One of the big problems we faced when we moved to LA was Tans's health. In the past, if she was unwell, it was all systems go to get back to Harefield Hospital for an appointment. There was a spell when we thought we wouldn't be able to live here in California.

Before Barack Obama came to power, we couldn't get medical insurance for Tans. Early on in this book, I talked about believing in fate. I believe things happen for a reason. We got her to LA and, around about the same time, all the insurance laws changed. For the first time, you could bring an existing illness to an insurance policy.

Since I made a career for myself in the movie business, that change in legislation was the biggest success we have had. We can talk about the movies and everything else that we've done but the health plan here, and health reforms, gave us the chance to get insurance to cover Tans so we could sleep more easily at night.

So now, if we have a problem, I just take her down the road to Cedars-Sinai Medical Center, with some of the best heart doctors in the world.

To give you an example, a friend of ours – Gorgeous George the medical actor (Adam Fogerty) – flew over on a £28 insurance deal on his VISA card. He got DVT and his bills ran into hundreds of thousands of dollars, but he was sorted.

Without cover over here, even to see the skin specialist, you have got to be a multimillionaire. If Tans went in for treatment, you're not talking hundreds of pounds or thousands: you're talking hundreds of thousands. So getting that sorted was a massive weight off our shoulders.

We get insurance through the Screen Actors' Guild. We pay a contribution but it's a fraction of what we would need to cough up if we had to cover the medical costs out of our own pocket.

When the British Heart Foundation (BHF) came to me in 2011, I was open to doing anything I could to help. We had done bits and pieces with Harefield and I had done a lot with other charities over the years but they said they wanted to do something a bit different to raise awareness of cardiopulmonary resuscitation, or CPR. They said they were thinking of doing this big movie-style campaign, very much like *Lock, Stock*.

All they asked for was two days of filming, and the dates fitted in fine with my diary. They sent me a script and I had a look through, reading all about the *Lock, Stock*-style characters and how they wanted it to feel like a movie. I was worried for a while beforehand that it would be cheesy – me playing a thug and larking about to the Bee Gees hit 'Stayin' Alive'.

We got down to filming in London and, as we were doing it, I could tell by the reaction that the guys behind it knew they had something special on their hands.

So it comes out on TV and, just like *Lock, Stock*, all of a sudden – and completely unexpectedly again – it goes boom! It just went through the roof and the reaction was incredible. Everyone said it was amazing, it was fantastic, it was funny. I think it has tipped over three million hits on YouTube. That's huge for a serious message about CPR. It reached a lot of people.

Once the advert hit cinemas and TV screens, then spread round the Internet, stories started to filter back to me. I heard within a week that a man's life had been saved. I couldn't get my head around it at first. You do these things, think, Job done, and then move on to something else. But suddenly I was getting emails from the UK about 'the Vinnie Jones advert saving my life'.

I was told a new statistic recently, that a life is saved every week because of the Vinnie Jones advert! I've played some big parts, but playing God? Of course I'm joking, but we are actually keeping people alive and it means the world that I have been involved, especially with Tans's story.

I am really overwhelmed with it, really proud. Every time I wake up in the morning, there are two or three Google alerts on my phone – 'Another man has been saved through the BHF Vinnie Jones advert. A little girl saved her mum. How did she know what to do? She watched Vinnie Jones's advert.'

Whenever people say, 'You have saved lives,' I don't see it like that. It's all about the brilliant people at the British Heart Foundation. They deserve the credit, not I. They came up with the idea, asked me to be involved and delivered a genius campaign. It was a brilliant idea and they got a great director who did things so well with a script by a very talented writer.

So you can take all the bad things that I've done, which seem to go in a cycle, but I've done my best to do some good too.

When the BHF came back to me and said they wanted to do the second in the series, I didn't hesitate. They said, 'There are twenty-eight other people who have been saved and we want to bring them in and put them in the same advert with you.'

I was quite laid back about it at the time, but then I walked into the studio and suddenly the emotion of it all hit me. I actually got in there and met all of them – shaking hands and looking into their eyes. It really hit home how amazing this whole thing was: the awareness we had created and the lives that were being saved. I used to get people making jokes in the street about squeezing Gazza's balls. Then people would say, 'It's been emotional' from *Lock, Stock*. Now, I think I get 'Ah, ah, ah, ah – stayin' alive!' sung at me like Barry bloody Gibb!

Hopefully, from the campaigns, we will get people to carry a donor card, give blood or even just learn how to do CPR. The message from me is simple – just help in any way you can. In my case, it has changed my life – and saved the lives of many others.

The upbeat message and all the goodwill in the world from the campaign was shattered for me in November 2011, though. I got a call to tell me my old Leeds United and Wales teammate Gary Speed had taken his own life.

Gary was a fluent Welsh speaker and taught me the words to the Welsh national anthem with John Hartson when I first got my international clearance through. I played the song on loop and drove everyone mad with my over-the-top singing, but Gary would just smile – as he always did – and laugh along with me. He'd be laughing now if he could hear all our Leeds stories again.

He will always hold a place dear to my heart because I remember singling him out in the match programme when I was playing at Elland Road. All the senior players would write a column about 'Ones to watch' and I chose Gary as a youngster.

He had everything – including speed: he jumped like a gazelle, he could head the ball, he had one of the best left foots in the game and had real composure. I remember the words very well: 'If he just keeps his head down and concentrates on his football he's going to be around a long, long time. He's going to be a household name.' I'm always proud that I got that right.

Whenever I saw him I would make him laugh. I wouldn't even have to say anything – the mischief was all over our faces. Speedo used to look up to me in those days, and I was the heart and soul of the dressing room for the young lads coming through. I talked them all through buying their first houses because they didn't really have a clue. I felt like a brother to that crop of players coming through. The words 'good influence' weren't always associated with my name during my playing days, but I'm sure Speedo would have called me just that, along with David Batty.

It's moments like Gary's tragic death that remind you how lucky you are to be here. Life is to be savoured.

All the more reason to make sure you know CPR.

Epilogue

I'm very proud of the fact that I'm a survivor.

A lot of people thought the Hollywood dream would last five minutes, that I'd be out in LA for a couple of movies and they would never hear of me again. It is exactly the same prejudice and attitude that followed me around as a footballer. Everyone thought I was destined to drop like a lead weight from the very top to non-League. But I didn't.

As I sit here writing this in my cabana on Mulholland Drive, I have sixty-five movies under my belt – not all of them are *Lock, Stock*s – three or four TV shows (one as a regular), and I feel established. It has been fifteen years of constant work in one of the most competitive industries in the world.

You look around at the moment and there are some great British stars making a brilliant living in TV and film in the US – guys like Jonny Lee Miller on *Elementary* and Hugh Laurie with *House*. I've had a great innings, too, but behind all of us there are tens of thousands who never get their break. Do I count my blessings every day? Too right I do.

My footballing days feel like a lifetime ago now. Every so often I will call up YouTube, especially if I'm away working, and look up some of the footage of the days at Leeds or that goal for Chelsea against Liverpool back in the day.

The thing is, as much as I love making movies, I still can't feel what I felt on the pitch. I can't replicate playing in front of the Elland Road crowd and how the hairs on the back of my neck would stand up when they sang my name. Or the elation of the moment when I banged one in at the Kop end at Anfield. Nothing compares. Those moments in my life are only memories now, which I savour, especially Wimbledon and the FA cup.

I find it hard to contemplate what has happened to me in my life – it really is against all the odds that things have worked out so well for me. Subconsciously, I've done my best to derail a brilliant set of cards delivered to me by fate, but that just makes me believe in destiny even more.

What I did yesterday is not what I want to do tomorrow. What I achieved yesterday is fine, but I want to achieve more tomorrow. I never wanted to be that bloke boring people at the bar with stories about winning the FA Cup. I know a lot of players and ex-players like that – and that's all they have to talk about.

The older generation of footballers could be very bitter and I didn't want that to happen to me. It really hurt me when I got into the Welsh squad and Leeds legend John Charles really dug me out. I'd met him a few times when he was down on his luck and I took him to a couple of dinners. I looked after him when he was skint. I genuinely loved the geezer and then he hammered me for playing for Wales because he believed you should qualify for selection only if your parents were Welsh. It disappointed me. I

Epilogue

felt sad more than angry. Trevor Brooking, who had been on my case on *Match of the Day*, calling me a thug and not a player, is another one sitting in an ivory tower – I was just trying to earn a living!

The game has moved on so much since I played, though. Footballers now are rock stars. They are the equivalent of A-list movie stars. It winds me up to hear criticism of guys like David Beckham, Wayne Rooney, John Terry or Frank Lampard earning more than a hundred grand a week.

Football is such a massive business. Compare it with movies and the music industry. I would argue sport is bigger than both of them put together now.

So why shouldn't a player be paid movie-star and rock-star money? I think fair play to them – they deserve every penny. Madonna or Sting could pocket $50 million for a tour. So, as far as I'm concerned, guys like A-Rod in baseball deserve their $180 million over ten years.

Look at Rory McIlroy in golf and his deal with Nike – he deserves every penny. I've tried to earn a bit more over the years with Red Devil energy drinks; I had my own range of jeans, TW Steel watches and I am a lifetime ambassador for Warrior now – I have cupboards full of caps, boots, T-shirts and hats. Why not? You've got to make hay while the sun shines. My old manager Peter Burrell used to joke with me about that. He'd say, 'Get the balaclava on, Vin, we're doing a smash-and-grab.' We'd turn up for a corporate event, get paid and get out. But I've always had the attitude that, if you earn £50, then you spend £50. There's no point being the richest man in the graveyard.

I'm coming up to my fiftieth birthday and I feel as if I've just about cracked it. I'm not drinking, all is good at home, my golf is steady and my Hollywood All Stars football team are top of the league. I've got the dog well and truly in the kennel.

Writing this book, with that beast tamed, I can look back at all the characters I've met through my life – footballers, geezers in the pubs and on the building sites, all the way through to actors – and I can see them struggling along with their dogs. It really tickles me because my big Alsatian, or big black wolf, is tucked away.

One of my best mates in the world, the first person I roomed with in football, was Wally Downes. He has been with me all the way through and has just spent three months living with us in LA. Wally has his own special place at the poker table in the cabana at my house. It can be dangerous in Hollywood: there are unscrupulous people about. But Wally is a great acid test for all of that.

I've reached a stage in my life where I am happiest having a party and dinner round at my house every weekend. I love people coming round, so I don't have to get out of my shorts. I am sociable and, I think, pretty generous, too. I love to have company and be around people.

The more the merrier as far as I am concerned. If Joe Kinnear, my manager at Wimbledon, said to get the boys out to boost the team spirit, I would be the one getting the lads out racing. If one or two of them said it wasn't really for them? Fuck off, it's all for one and one for all in football. On Saturday we're all together. Whether Terry Phelan is at left back or David Beckham is at right midfield, you'll want him to come and help you on Saturday afternoon if he's your teammate.

I say to my boys now, at Hollywood All Stars FC, 'Just stay half an hour and have a social drink with the boys. Have orange or lemonade or have ten pints, just be a team.'

And here's the thing – I need that team. I need that to help me with the big dog. Without them around, he would break the chain and be pulling me along with him.

It's not just the team: I have always needed a manager figure in my life to keep me on the straight and narrow. My son would have a military analogy for it: I'm not the general, more of a captain or a major, keeping the team together. But I always have to have a general to give me that guidance. Over the years my granddad Arthur, my dad, Dave Bassett, Joe Kinnear, Frenchie, Howard Wilkinson, Peter Burrell and recently Alex Cole have all been there for me with that guidance. I'll for ever be indebted for what they have done for me, especially when that bloody dog has gone on the rampage.

People ask me all the time if I would ever go back to Britain or make a return to football management, but there's nothing there for me now. My family love coming over to LA – and we sacrificed a lot to take the plunge in another country. Don't get me wrong: I love England, Scotland, Ireland and Wales – I'm very passionate about it. But it's not the Britain I remember growing up in. It's changed dramatically now.

We've adapted in the way that my friends now come here. I have friends come here on a Thursday and go home on a Sunday – we're not in the Stone Age any more. You jump on a plane, you leave Heathrow at midday and you're here at 3 p.m. on the same day because of the time difference. It's fantastic.

I don't have any plans to take my foot off the gas; I love the cut and thrust of working in Hollywood. I've still got enough in the tank to live life in the fast lane. I've just done a movie with Christian Slater in Canada, which was signed off on the same afternoon I was putting pen to paper on a deal for another film. All on the same afternoon I went to see Victor Morton, the psychologist, to keep that dog under control.

I can't believe my luck some days. Recently we were out for dinner at Chateau Marmont and some famous face came over and said, 'Hey, Vinnie. How you doing?' I had to ask Kaley who it was and she told me it was Josh Brolin!

Wally took me under his wing at Wimbledon and we're still mates nearly thirty years on. Tanya always says I don't have to pay everybody back, but I feel I do. If anybody has done me a good turn, I will always be there.

There is a good test of a man, which I stand by to this day. If it's 3 a.m. and pouring down with rain and your car breaks down, who are the first people who spring to mind that you're going to ring for help? How many of the people in your phone do you think would say, 'I'm on my way right now' – no excuses, just 100 per cent commitment? I feel incredibly lucky to have seven or eight. Some people may not even have one.

I said to Tanya recently that it was a special year for us, making it to 2013, because my endowment policy matured – 25 years since I got my first mortgage.

I always remember buying that house near John Barnes and loads of other footballers on that estate in Hemel. I can picture the day in 1988 thinking, How the fuck am I gonna pay for this? I committed to £125,000 for it, which was a fortune compared with what I was earning back then – about £300 a week.

I said to myself, 'Fuck me, I'm going to be nearly fifty when this is paid off!' It seemed more like 150 years in the future. My mum lives there now.

If you had told her all those years ago when I stormed out of the house with all my possessions in a bin liner that one day I would be a happily married actor in Hollywood, she would have laughed. We all would have laughed.

But that's life, isn't it? So, up to now, it's been emotional.

Acknowledgements

Thanks to 'Sweaty' aka Gordon Smart from the *Sun* for writing this book with me; and for all the hard work he has put in. A good mate over the years and a regular fixture in our cabana in LA. As for the missed penalty for the Hollywood Allstars and the booking in the first five minutes, we'll leave that out of the book shall we?

Picture credits

The author and publishers would like to thank the following copyright-holders for permission to reproduce images in this book:

© News Syndication: 3, 4, 5, 6, 12, 13

© Mirrorpix: 7, 9, 10

© Getty Images: 8, 17, 18, 19, 21, 22, 24, 29

© Rex Features: 11, 15, 16, 20, 23, 25, 26, 45

© BBC Photo Library: 27

© 20th Century Fox: 28

Reproduced by kind permission of the British Heart Foundation, and the 'Hands-Only CPR' campaign: 37

All other images are care of the author.

The author and publishers have made all reasonable efforts to contact copyright-holders for permission, and apologise for any omissions or errors in the form of credits given. Corrections may be made for future printings.